DIVINE DESIGN

DIVINE DESIGN

BY CAROL DONAYRE BUGG, ASID, DDCD

DECORATING DEN'S 25TH ANNIVERSARY COLLECTION

FOREWORD BY MARIO BUATTA

ISBN 0-939596-1-1

Produced for Decorating Den Systems, Inc.

by Judd Publishing Inc./Kathleen Hughes, Bookbuilders

Designed by Anne Masters Design, Inc.

Printed in Singapore

DEDICATION

TO THE WOMEN IN MY LIFE...

• MY BEAUTIFUL MOTHER, WHO IN HER LIFETIME CONTINUALLY EXPOSED ME TO GOOD DESIGN, INDIVIDUAL STYLE, AND THE INCOMPARABLE ENERGY OF MANHATTAN.

• MY DEAR SISTER JEANNE, WITH WHOM I SHARE THOSE PASSIONS LEARNED FROM MOTHER.

• MY DARLING DAUGHTERS; KAREN, DARLENE, AND WHITNEY, WHO ARE THE BEST PRESENTS MY HUSBAND EVER GAVE ME.

• TO ALL THE LOVELY AND TALENTED WOMEN ASSOCIATED WITH DECORATING DEN... BEGINNING WITH THE OUTSTANDING ROLE MODELS AT THE CORPORATE OFFICE.

• MY EBULLIENT FRIEND, PATTI COONS, AND HER ASSOCIATES, JILL LOCHTE AND PAULA TRANFAGLIA; EACH OF WHOM MAKES MY LIFE A LITTLE EASIER. MY VERY SPECIAL THANKS TO PAULA FOR HER INTREPID ATTENTION TO THE DETAILS OF GETTING *DIVINE DESIGN* PUBLISHED.

• TO ALL DECORATING DEN INTERIOR DECORATORS, FOR THEIR DEDICATION TO BEAUTIFY-ING THE LIVES OF THEIR CLIENTS. MY SINCEREST THANKS TO EACH DECORATOR EXTRAOR-DINAIRE WHOSE WORK APPEARS IN *DIVINE DESIGN*.

CONTENTS

FOREWORD

I WAS SO EXCITED when I first learned that Carol was preparing a book to commemorate Decorating Den's 25th anniversary. In 1990 I participated in Decorating Den's annual Dream Room Contest, held in my stomping grounds of New York City at the landmark Plaza Hotel. It was then that I had the opportunity to preview a selection of magnificent Decorating Den room makeovers. We have had a longstanding mutual admiration ever since!

Over the years, through three Dream Room Contests, speaking at the 1990 Washington, D.C. market conference and even enjoying dinner with the Decorating Den gang and 1993 Decorator of the Year, Judith Slaughter, I have learned of many similarities between myself and Decorating Den interior decorators. Although our clients may differ in various ways from budget to design...one very important element is the same... clients who think they can find that particular piece or get that fabric or treatment cheaper elsewhere! No matter what the budget range on a project...this decorator nightmare is a universal problem.

We also share many positive aspects of the home design industry. Such as the great feeling of accomplishment when you look at the completed project, only to have this reinforced by an ecstatic client!

As a child, I loved the "lived in" quality of my aunt's home, a home filled with objects and discoveries from many countries and times, a scrapbook of her life collecting. In contrast my family's house was an all-white modern home lacking in personality and charm. I suppose this is why I relate so well to Decorating Den and its philosophy of incorporating one's lifestyle into decorating and design. For these are the true elements of making a house a home.

Interior design is the creative medium by which homeowners/clients display their personalities. Each one of us wants to surround ourselves with a living environment that is reflective of our lifestyle. Unfortunately, many still carry the picture of decorators from days gone by. These decorators did not consider the client's lifestyle when working on a project, only the end result, its grandeur and their egos! Decorating Den has broken this mold.

With the fast-paced lifestyle of today's world, needing the services of an interior decorator is not uncommon. Locating and procuring the services of a successful decorator will save not only time and frustration, but in the long run, money! Getting the job done right the first time is the key. How many of us have set out on our own redecorating project with less than full conviction of exactly what we hope to achieve, only to change our minds midstream, or never complete the project!

As a result of the extravagant 1980's, the 1990's introduced the trend of "cocooning." Many of us are choosing to stay home for quality entertainment and family life. Today's stressful, busy world makes the relaxing, secure environments of our homes much more appetizing. Whether you seek the tranquility of cool serene hues or vibrant festive colors for a lively awakening decor, your home not only displays your personality but also provides a nurturing cocoon.

The difference between an average interior decorator and a GREAT interior decorator is the ability to design around a client's lifestyle, budget and taste. The following pages are full of wonderful stories that reflect this type of client/decorator relationship.

I suggest you find a comfortable chair, and sit back for a relaxing emersion into a 25 year celebration of real life decorating which will prove to be both informative and inspirational!

Congratulations, Decorating Den! You've only just begun...

Mario Buatta

THE DECORATING DEN STORY

Ten years ago I attended the summer program of the Parsons School of Design in Paris. As an interior decorator and an avowed Francophile, Paris and Parsons was an unbeatable combination. While I was enjoying those carefree adult student days, I remember worrying that when I returned home everything would seem anticlimactic. I could never have anticipated the new direction my life was about to take.

Some would say it was luck, and others would swear it was destiny. Louis Pasteur stated it best, "Chance favors the prepared mind." With my design background, and my husband Jim's knowledge of franchising, we were ready for the opportunity that was about to come our way.

One day as Jim was waiting to get his hair cut he found himself leafing through a *Woman's Day* magazine. Life's timing could not have been more propitious. Jim's attention was captured by a story about a woman who owned a Decorating Den franchise.

Even though Jim and I had thought about franchising interior decorators, we had never been clever enough to come up with the Decorating Den ColorVan® concept.

It hardly seems a decade since Jim and I met with Steve and Valerie Bursten, the founders of Decorating Den. The Burstens were certainly ahead of the times with this innovative interior decorating concept. My husband and I, now the owners of Decorating Den, are proud to carry on the traditions set by the founders of this unique interior decorating company.

Decorating Den founders Steve and Valerie Bursten giving Jim his first ride in a ColorVan

WHAT IS DECORATING DEN?

The Burstens' concept seems simple now, but at the time it was quite revolutionary. For entrepreneurs who want to turn their talent and love of decorating into owning their own business, Decorating Den offers a grand vehicle. For consumers looking for an affordable and comfortable way to have beautifully decorated rooms, Decorating Den is a shop on wheels that conveniently services the customer at home.

THE INTERIOR DECORATING SERVICE

Decorating Den is the first affordable, international, shop-at-home interior decorating service. Each franchise is owned by a professionally trained interior decorator who brings thousands of samples of fabric, wallcovering, carpet, and catalogs of furniture and accessories directly to their customer in a completely stocked ColorVan®. The customer enjoys the convenience, at no charge, of reviewing generous samples in the lighting conditions which exist in their own home or office.

Decorating Den specializes in working with customers moving into or redecorating a home, office, or retail location by designing around the client's personality and lifestyle.

THE FRANCHISE STORY

Decorating Den combines two of the late twentieth century's hottest trends: franchising and women in business. Ninety-eight percent of the franchises are owned by women. We are also on the cutting edge of another of today's directions: husbands and wives whose dream is to work together. Most regional franchises are husband and wife teams.

Franchisees with Decorating Den are offered an outstanding and ongoing educational program. Besides the traditional study of interior design, franchisees learn in depth all about their products, marketing skills, sales techniques, and most importantly, the systems for running a successful business. Franchisees are given many career enhancement opportunities. One is an optional two day exam that qualifies those who pass to the appellate, DDCD (Decorating Den Certified Decorator.)

A DECORATING DEN SCRAPBOOK

Here are some of the highlights of a decade of extraordinary events at Decorating Den.....

Television Decorating Den has had national coverage on all the major T.V. networks. Our first exposure was on the NBC "TODAY" Show with an interview at the International Home Furnishings Show in High Point, N.C. The ABC "HOME" Show and Decorating Den combined forces for a $75,000 Sweepstakes. CBS's "THIS MORNING" Show selected Decorating Den to do a makeover project.

NBC "TODAY" Show interview at High Point, N.C. Home Furnishings Show

Live on the ABC "HOME" Show with Host Gary Collins and Decorating Editor Kitty Bartholomew

First Lady's Luncheon Once a year in the Nation's Capitol, United States Congressional Wives honor the First Lady with a special luncheon. Former First Lady Barbara Bush was the inspiration for the design and colors of the fabric that was used for the tablecloths at one of the luncheons. I worked with Waverly to create the exclusive Decorating

Harry Smith, Host of "CBS This Morning" previewing room makeover with decorator Sharon Spring

Den pattern. This popular fabric has also been used at Presidential dinners, an elegant affair at Sothebys in New York, and continues to be a part of many State Department diplomatic receptions. There will be a new Decorating Den exclusive design for the next First Lady's Luncheon in honor of First Lady Hillary Rodham Clinton.

First Lady Barbara Bush and Marilyn Quayle at the head table draped in our exclusive "First Lady Fabric" unveiled at the 1990 First Lady's Luncheon

Woman's Day Contest

Once again *Woman's Day* makes an impact on Decorating Den. We joined forces to sponsor a Dream Bedroom Makeover Contest. Over 6,000 entries were received. The three winners are featured in Divine Design's chapter on master bedrooms.

Over 6,000 entries were received for the Women's Day Dream Bedroom Makeover Contest

Reviewing entries at Woman's Day in New York with Decorating Editor Pam Abrahams

Leader Dogs for the Blind® Proceeds from the sale of an exclusive Decorating Den fabric that was inspired by my late faithful companion, Partner, go to support Decorating Den's national charity, Leader Dogs for the Blind®. Established in 1939, Leader Dogs for the Blind® assists the visually impaired by teaming them up with guide dogs.

Leader Dogs for the Blind graduate Elizabeth Parkhurst with Abigail

Decorating Den Conferences And Trips Each year Decorating Den holds a fun-filled and educational market conference at a fabulous hotel. The Princess in Acapulco, Bally's in Las Vegas, and The Dolphin in Orlando are but a few. One of the highlights is the awards banquet where franchisees and regions are recognized for their outstanding achievements. In addition to the social functions, Decorating Den sets up an expansive market featuring our latest products, decorated model rooms, pre-conference schools and workshops, and speakers such as the renowned Dr. Joyce Brothers, the acclaimed textile designer Jay Yang, and decorator extraordinaire Mario Buatta. Decorating Den also periodically sponsors special trips to dream cities, such as, Marbella, Spain; Cancun, Mexico; and Paris, France.

Textile designer Jay Yang previewing his latest fabrics with the Carolinas Regional Director Linda Riddiough

1993 Decorator of the Year Judith Slaughter sharing her Dream Room entry with Mario Buatta

Dream Room Contest Decorating Den promotes their interior decorators in an Annual Dream Room contest. The decorators' entries are taken to the world-renowned Plaza Hotel in New York City for judging. Here the decorators are given an unprecedented opportunity to have their work seen by an illustrious group of editors from national media. Over the years, participating magazines have included: *House Beautiful, Woman's Day, Home, HG, Better Homes and Gardens*, and *Metropolitan Home*. Pictures of the rooms have appeared in many of the above magazines, and Charles Gandee featured Decorating Den in his "At Large" column in *HG*, June, 1991. In addition, Kitty Bartholomew displayed the winning entries on the ABC "HOME" Show.

Our illustrious Dream Room judges from HG, Home, ABC "HOME" Show, Woman's Day, to name a few

At one of these judgings, our 1991 Decorator of the Year, Terri Ann Parks, was introduced to Donald Trump, the owner of the Plaza Hotel. Mr. Trump was so

Donald Trump and Terri Ann Parks with my favorite PR person Patti Coons

impressed with Decorating Den and Terri that he asked her to redecorate the Plaza's Presidential Suite! Terri's prestigious job was a direct result of Decorating Den's Dream Room Contest. Now the Presidential Suite is the site of our annual judging, and the place where each new Decorator of the Year is given the royal treatment.

The redecorated living room of the Presidential Suite, Plaza Hotel, N.Y.C.

Paris Redux The last entry in my Decorating Den scrapbook is one of my fondest memories of this past decade. I was able to return to Paris with a group of Decorating Den interior decorators, who shared my enthusiasm for the very things I had enjoyed when I was a student there ten years before... tours of Versailles, the Louvre, and the Musée D'Orsay...antiquing at the famous Paris flea market...class with one of my former teachers at the Musée Des Arts Décoratifs...shopping at the Galleries Lafayette...sipping aperitifs at the Café de la Paix...sightseeing at the famous Paris Opera House, Montmartre, Sacre Coeur, Notre Dame, and the Eiffel Tower... and the grand finale, dining and dancing aboard the Bateau Mouche!

Back to Paris with a group of Dec Den franchise owners!

THE DECORATING DEN DIFFERENCE
FOR YOU

Inevitably at various stages of your life you will find yourself contemplating decorating one or more areas of your home. You might put it off because of those dreaded decorating demons, the terrible T's and the challenging C's.

TIME Too busy with work and family to devote the time to do the job properly.

TROUBLE Going from store to store collecting samples seems like more trouble than it's worth.

TALENT The burden of having to make all of the decisions for new furnishings is frightening, but you think that working with an interior decorator will present a whole new set of demons.

The most important benefit that Decorating Den provides the consumer is service. Decorating Den interior decorators own their own business, and are there to save the customer time, energy and money. They take pride in meeting their client's decorating needs. Things can go wrong in any business, but the Decorating Den owner takes care of those problems, and makes sure that in the end the customer is totally satisfied.

CONTROL It is true that a lot of interior decorators have a definite look that they pass on to customers whether it is their lifestyle or not.

THE DECORATING DEN DIFFERENCE Your home should look like you. At our first meeting we spend time learning about you — how you live, your style and color preferences.

CONVENIENCE Most often you are required to visit the shop or office of an interior decorator.

THE DECORATING DEN DIFFERENCE Our ColorVan® — stocked with thousands of samples will come right to your home, where you can see a variety of samples in your own lighting, with your own furnishings and colors.

CHANGE With utter disdain, many decorators are rather imperious when it comes to telling you what you have to get rid of.

COST Traditionally, interior decorators do not make free house calls. They charge hourly fees, or design fees in addition to the cost of the products. Generally, it is difficult to find someone who will take on a small job.

THE DECORATING DEN DIFFERENCE We work around the furnishings you already have and want to keep.

THE DECORATING DEN DIFFERENCE We know you are on a budget, that you like some of your current furnishings, that you want an advisor, not a dictator. We respect your limits and delight in your expectations. No job is too small, and our consultation is always complimentary.

We are committed to your needs: you must be able to hire a professional decorator who for a realistic budget is able to provide you with beauty, comfort and good design. Most importantly, when any Decorating Den project is completed, it should reflect you and your way of life.

And now, on to *Divine Design* and the work of Decorating Den's talented decorators. There is no better way to see for yourself what Decorating Den can do for you...as a customer, or as a decorator with a flair for business.

LIVING &
DINING ROOMS

EXPECTING COMPANY MIGHT BE THE MOTIVATION FOR DECORATING YOUR LIVING AND DINING ROOMS, BUT THESE ROOMS SHOULD NOT BE DECORATED FOR YOUR COMPANY. TOO OFTEN

PEOPLE PUT ALL OF THEIR DECORATING DOLLARS HERE AND END UP WITH SHOWPLACES THAT ARE USED ONLY FOR SPECIAL OCCASIONS. WHAT A WASTE! NEITHER YOU NOR YOUR GUESTS WILL FEEL COMFORTABLE IN ROOMS WORTHY OF A MUSEUM, OR DESIGNED SOLELY TO PLEASE VISITORS. YOU NEED THESE ROOMS TO BE SUITABLE FOR THE ENJOYMENT OF YOUR DAILY LIFE. LET YOUR PERSONALITY, YOUR INTERESTS, AND YOUR STYLE BE YOUR DECORATING GUIDES.

SOMEWHERE BETWEEN PARIS & PROVENCE

My living room combines old and new, real and fake, town and country, classic and modern, antiques and flea market finds... all blended together to create my own style, which is somewhere between Paris and Provence.

I fell in love with this room eighteen years ago. At first sight, I adored its gracious dimensions, high ceilings, classic wall moldings, large French windows and doors, and refined, but elegant fireplace. In my passion, I totally overlooked the room's weaknesses; awkward placement of one of the windows, old radiators, exposed hot water pipes, and challenging wall space. For years I considered drastic remodeling plans.

Then one day it came to me that accepting and making the most of what you already have is what love is all about. So I set out to devise a plan that would complement the good features of the room, and play down those that were not quite so pleasing.

The room's generous proportions and scale called for dramatic colors and accents. I began by covering the white walls with a tawny-hued strié paper that highlighted the molding. As my taste changed and when I was lucky enough to find the right

Laura Chandler's folding screen rendition of Paris beautifully camouflages an un-needed window.

piece at the right price, I would replace my old furnishings; but the furniture arrangement has basically remained the same.

Bergères and fauteuils, closed arm and open arm wood framed chairs in the style of Louis XV, mix with more contemporary upholstered pieces to create adaptable conversational groupings. The room works well for our large family gatherings and Decorating Den parties. It is equally suitable for entertaining just a few friends, or to enjoy all by myself.

A sophisticated Paris style blends well with the more relaxed charms associated with Provence. The black floral needlepoint rug smoothly bridges the decorating between town and country. So do the soft draperies with elegant tasseled tiebacks, and the charming portrait of a French peasant girl.

A Niermann Weeks mirror over the fireplace complements the classic lines of the decorative wall molding. Sitting on a radiator, framed by the exposed pipes and hiding a badly placed window is a folding screen painted by Laura Chandler. Now I always have a favorite view of Paris on my moveable feast!

At the end of most days you will find me sitting by the front window, enjoying two of my greatest pleasures; listening to music and catching up on my books and magazines.

Favorite photos and personal mementos provide the perfect background for a romantic celebration à deux.

CHANGING WITH THE SEASONS

Spring...lilac, peony pink with a dash of sky blue

Autumn...cinnamon and butterscotch hues

Winter...deep teal with rich wine as major colors

Summer...pine green complemented by geranium red

Calgary, Alberta is home to decorator Vianne Stein. She ascribes her unique living room designs to an occupational hazard. "As soon as I get our home decorated, I become restless and want to change it. I came up with an idea that has worked for my ever-changing moods...Seasons!"

Empty nesters, Vianne and her husband Brian designed their living room to be used, and to be the center of main floor activity. Colors of furniture, walls and carpet were kept neutral to provide a backdrop for her seasonal color changes. The focal point window gets the most dramatic seasonal changes, and all done with the magic of velcro. Even pillows have velcro closures for instant change, easy storage and less expense. Best of all, Vianne never has a chance to tire of the current look, before it is time to introduce the next season.

PICASSO AND PATTERN

C. Delle Bates purchased a 1950's cottage style home so he could have a place for showcasing his art and collectibles. The collection includes Picassos, original paintings by Francois Guilot (Picasso's first wife), as well as other renowned contemporary artists, and African and Haitian sculptures. Not sure of which came first, his love of Picasso or his love of pattern, C. Delle gave Texas decorator Becky Aleman the job of combining both passions in his living room.

She began by making some substantial background changes. The original wood paneling was painted a striking peacock, and an earthy Mexican saltillo tile was chosen for the floor. Next, Becky selected a mixture of exuberant patterns in vibrant tones that would emulate the strong colors of C. Delle's collection.

C. Delle Bates's colorful collection of art and furnishings was given an exciting peacock backdrop.

Large scale pottery lamps add further drama.

A sense of serenity was created by Beverly Richards with trompe l'oeil lattice and ivy.

Before

Before

Malibu colors replace 1950's earth tones in Beverly Nesmith's room, below.

With a wash of purple paint Tina Reyburn changed the look of the above fireplace.

Before

FABULOUS FIREPLACE RE-DOS!

There is nothing like a fireplace to warm up a room. Here are three living rooms, transformed from average to fabulous by their new focal point — the fireplace painted in a fresh new color! Canadian interior decorator Beverley Richards wanted a living room that was "a sanctuary where one can feel at peace with one's self." She achieved this serenity by lightening up the fireplace and hearth with pale faux finish that is repeated on the walls. A trompe l'oeil lattice and ivy design create a sense of endless space and peace.

Fresh new paint transformed the simple brick fireplace in this California ranch house, decorated by Tina Reyburn with her client's artwork in mind. She chose sparkling jewel tones for the new fabrics, and painted the fireplace in a tint of purple, neither too dark and distracting, nor too soft and washed-out.

The client's favorite painting decided decorator Beverly Nesmith to replace 1950's earth tones with a Malibu color scheme. The pale neutral background and sponge-painted fireplace, the floating curvilinear sofa, and the tropical accents bring this now sumptuous California living room out of the Dark Ages.

THE BOLD AND
THE BEAUTIFUL

Empty nesters often either dispose of all their old furniture and start over, or keep their old familiar furnishings, but spruce them up. When empty nesters Joyce and Bob Taylor down-sized to a condo, they blended the best of both scenarios, keeping the majority of their furniture, but opting for a real color awakening. Thanks to Michigan decorator Carol Sanborn, the Taylors' living room is awash with brilliant color, the perfect example of how to bring new life to old familiar furnishings.

Carol papered the walls to give the room warmth and accent the architectural details. Then she added a valance to balance and blend the arched window into the room. Attention to detail is everywhere: from the carefully framed pictures to the colorful pillows and accessories.

The corner cut-outs of the valance allow the trim to show.

Before color awakening.

The glass cocktail table with graceful verdigris legs sits on a custom-crafted area rug.

A vibrant new wall color accents the architectural details, and draws attention to the pictures and accessories.

*Opposite, the dramatic look of cool
white-on-white is warmed by touches of
sophisticated dark tones.*

CONTEMPORARY CLASSICS

*Lush textures accent the elegant new
green marble fireplace hearth, above.*

*Do you remember seeing pictures of
those all-white rooms that were in
vogue in the 1930's? High society
decorator Syrie Maugham began
this trend that was all the rage with
the smart set. Hollywood followed
suit with luxurious white-on-white
sets designed by MGM art director
Cedric Gibbons. Most people did not
dare to copy this expensive and
impractical look associated with
movies and millionaires. Times have
changed. Luxury and high style are
no longer the prerogative of
Hollywood and the wealthy alone.
Whatever your heart desires, in the
way of decorating, it is within reach.
Take white. During the 1980's enor-
mous strides were made in protective
coatings both for fabrics and carpet,
which has made upkeep relatively
simple and maintenance free. Even
better, with the choice of luxurious
well-priced fabrics available on
today's market, everyone can afford
to live in elegant surroundings.*

Interior decorator Lois Pade, DDCD, designed a luxurious white-on-white dramatic look for the octagon-shaped living room of her Wisconsin clients. Sophisticated colors and accessories heighten the impact and warm up the cool whites. The window design is both striking and practical. Pleated shades provide privacy when required, along with light control, and protection from the cold Northern winters. Formal swags in a dramatic print and delicate tassels top off the windows. Long white panels complete the exquisite window treatment.

Sharon Knox helped her California clients completely re-do their living room. The remodeling included adding new windows, custom cabinetry and a wrap-around window seat. Lush textures in silvery blues and hyacinth commingle with a midnight tapestry print and the elegant new green marble fireplace hearth. The mirror doubles the effect of the prized Hong vases.

GREAT LOCATIONS

In real estate parlance the three most important criteria for selecting a house are location, location, location. Illinois decorator Lynnay Kallemeyn gave Debbie Manderino's "track-home-tiny" house, a whole new look when she decided to stay because of its proximity to her business. The Maurice Prendergast print inspired the "old world" ambience, reflecting Debbie's new traditional tastes. Lynnay arranged the classic Queen Anne style cherry furniture and plush transitional loveseats for intimate conversation, adding a desk for household correspondence. Walls and carpet became tones of Aegean green, while an antique wood framed screen upholstered in a black and white Toile de Jouy, a carved Louis XV embellishment over a pair of classic fruit prints, and an area-defining needlepoint rug pull living and dining rooms together in her small, but oh so gracious home!

Barbara and Dickie Andrews decided to completely renovate their 1912 house instead of moving. New living room decor was vital, since the front door opens directly into it, and it doubles as a showroom for Barbara's interior decorating clients. She chose dark Bordeaux red for the walls, recovered her antique camelback sofa in a bold floral fabric, and added white antique satin swags with a red lining and a floral hint on the border.

An intimate arrangement of a choice selection of furnishings allows space for a desk.

The colors and similar "Old World" ambience pull the living room and adjacent dining room together.

There is a rich contrast between the white antique satin swags and the vibrant impact of the dark Bordeaux red walls.

LAKESIDE LIVING

When Tom and Nora Hughes moved from fast-paced New York City to southern Charlotte, North Carolina, this light-filled house, with their new boat at the back door floating on Lake Norman, made the transition to a less formal lifestyle very easy. Mixing their eclectic old furniture with new, decorator Myra Carter created this casually charming dining room and two-story great room, appropriate to the lakeside setting. Starting with a pair of sea foam green chairs and the white sectional sofa, she planned an emerald, ruby, and white color palette for the two rooms, and anchored both with jewel-toned bordered area rugs. Two coordinating printed fabrics cover pillows, Parsons side chairs and the windows to complete the sophisticated yet comfortable feeling in the living room.

In the dining room the brilliant new colors and rich patterns have given a whole new lease on life to the Hughes' handsome oak furniture. Picking up on her clients' new hobby, Myra introduced a subtle hint of the nautical in the rope design on the chair fabric, in the rug's ruby border, and with the gold cord and tassels that dress the table.

Jewel-toned fabrics and colors rejuvenate the Hughes' oak dining room furniture.

Two comfortable chairs brought from the Hughes' previous house flank the fireplace.

When windows are exposed to a beautiful water view, or any pleasant vista, there is a tendency to want to leave them bare. However, people forget how cold a wall of glass can look at night. Myra's solution was to dress the very top of the windows with an elegant throw swag. Rather than detract from the view, the color, pattern, and simple design of the treatment enhance the dramatic wall of windows.

An eclectic mixture of furnishings is anchored by a jewel-toned bordered area rug. A soft swag accents the wall of windows.

COZY CORNERS

Here are three lovely spaces, each one with its own unique charm and flair. The first is in a lovely Illinois home, where decorator Cindy Schweisthal, DDCD, created an ideal Victorian setting for enjoying afternoon tea. Contrasting cranberries and evergreens against pristine white, and rich dark woods and tapestry with satin and lace give this treasure-filled living room its grace.

Ohio decorator Patricia Cripe has taken advantage of the generous bay window in her own dining room by filling it with a camelback loveseat. Chairseats have been recovered in a coordinating pattern. The simple, but unusual window treatment with its gilded brackets adds a final touch of panache.

The elegant, yet accessible look of this small dining area was decorated by Anne Allred, DDCD. A sumptuous spruce green silky flamestitch tableskirt is overlayed with trimmed and tasseled tapestry. This dining space may be small, but it is big on Texas charm.

This treasure-filled living room corner is the ideal setting for afternoon tea.

A sumptuous skirted table creates an elegant dining area.

A dining room bay window surrounds this camelback love seat.

SOUTHERN CHARM

Shirley Legum knew that she wanted a cozy, feminine, flower-filled room; but she did not know where to start. When she called in Georgia interior decorator Terri Ervin, Shirley loved Terri's suggestions, from the exquisite window treatment design, to the clever glass-top ottoman coffee table, to the leafy green accents that added relief to the rose color scheme. But, when Terri recommended painting the white walls a sunny golden tone, Shirley said emphatically, "No!" Terri's conviction that this one detail would take the room from the minor into the major leagues, finally convinced her client. Shirley is the first to admit that she never believed how much difference painting the walls would make.

When it came to the adjacent dining room, Shirley wanted it formal, but asked Terri to work around her husband's inherited set of casual furniture. Room changes began with the introduction of several coordinating floral chintzes. A second degree of formality was achieved by adding a pair of skirted upholstered chairs. The rose palette, and a richly swagged window treatment complete the pretty new picture.

Favorite pictures and fond memories decorate the antique lady's writing desk.

Floral chintz and upholstered chairs bring a touch of formality to the set of casual furniture.

Painting the walls a sunny gold made
all the difference to this charming
living room.

In any sport the best amateur who
"plays" at the game can never quite
match the professional who makes
a living at it. The same holds true
for interior decoration. Many people have a flair for design, but their
ability to pull a room together falls
short of what a professional decorator can accomplish. It is not only
the resources available to those in
the business, it is their discerning
eye and experience that take a room
out of the ordinary.

BREAKING WITH TRADITION

When it comes to decorating, being able to start from scratch can be a mixed blessing. When the Finnells faced this situation they called in Massachusetts ASID Allied Member decorator, Robin Cotter, who laid out an overall plan to save them hours of frustration, not to mention hundreds of dollars.

One of Karen Finnell's main concerns was where to place an ebony baby grand piano she anticipated receiving. Another, was how to break away from their strictly traditional decorating style. First Robin listened to ideas for decorating their living room. Then she set out to fulfill those dreams.

Green walls set the color tone for the eclectic mix of furniture and accessories. Classic furniture mixes well with the contemporary glass-and-wrought iron cocktail table, and the corner torchere. The needlepoint area rug and softly draped table lend an air of genteel sophistication.

The dining room was another story. Here the Finnells wanted to keep a more traditional look to blend with the built-in corner cabinets, wainscoting and Queen Anne furniture. The room also had to coordinate with the living room.

The lush patterns and tones of the living room, as well as the simply elegant asymmetric window treatments are repeated in the gracious traditional dining room.

Here is a living room where classic successfully mingles with contemporary. Pleasing colors and textures add to the sophisticated ambience.

LE PETIT PARKS

The dining room in the Presidential Suite of the Plaza Hotel, New York City, which Terri Ann Parks decorated.

A common question that decorators often hear is, "How can I make my room look larger?" Texas interior decorator, Terri Ann Parks, 1991 Decorator of the Year, recently faced that challenge in her own home, after she finished decorating the largest space of her career: the 12,000 square feet of the Presidential Suite at New York's Plaza Hotel! Four of Terri's dining rooms could easily have fit into the suite's spacious one. But Terri captured the same charm and elegant ambience associated with grander rooms in a scale suitable to her petite space.

Terri's first step in opening up the room was to install a larger window. Then she visually doubled the space by mirroring an entire wall, with a unique white wood detailing. Silk wisteria and grapevines draw your eye up the burgundy walls to lovely dentil molding at the ceiling. Terri knew that painting the room this dark dramatic color would visually raise the ceiling and heighten the drama. And lastly, the romantic arched top window treatment completes the look of luxury for Le Petit Parks.

Terri Ann Park's beautifully appointed dining room in her Houston home, where an exceptionally beautiful glass-topped table enhances the open feeling and reflects the tapestry fabric on the fully upholstered chairs and the custom beveled bordered rug, all illumined by a luxurious crystal chandelier with silk shades and a fabric cord cover.

Traditional elegance fills interior decorator Judith Slaughter's lovely dining room.

A ROOM FOR ALL SEASONS

The table is set for a glorious April luncheon.

1993 Decorator of the Year Judith Slaughter, DDCD, described her own dining room as, "the shoemaker's child...boring, and the window treatments looked tired. It needed spirit-lifting pattern and color. I wanted it to sing with exuberant color," said Judith. One cold, gray February day, she began plotting her new decorating scheme.

Working around her lovely Queen Anne furniture and fine oriental rug, Judith Slaughter selected a wallcovering that combined sunshine yellow and flowers on the vine. Then she picked a vibrant red, green and yellow plaid to recover her dining room chairs, and for a beautiful swag and jabot treatment at the windows.

At a glorious April luncheon, the room's brilliant new colors and patterns sing, along with the first flowers and fruit of the season. But this all-season dining room provides an equally warm and inviting setting for entertaining in every month.

Gracious accessories add to the room's inviting appearance.

FORMAL AND
INFORMAL COUNTRY

Before she became a professional decorator, Kathy Dyer, DDCD, made a wallcovering mistake and lived with it for five years. Now Kathy's dramatic dark hunter green floral paper has revived both her room and her spirits. The new wallcovering inspired the delicious bordered area rug. A classic Waverly pattern coordinates the delicate gathered valances for the triple French doors with matching ruffled cushions for her chairs. The room suggests country, but with a touch of formality.

The Floyds hired New Jersey decorator Dawn Hladkey to give their dining room a great new informal country look. They believed in Dawn's professional ability to pull it all together — despite their original reluctance to use pattern. Now subtle stencil patterned wallpaper and border coordinate with the popular Waverly red and cream print. The stencil design is repeated in each corner of the custom area rug. With Dawn's finishing touches of wrought iron tiebacks, custom chair pads with large bows, and a new chandelier, this is a dining room the Floyds are proud of.

The stencil design of the wallpaper is echoed in the custom bordered area rug. Dawn Hladkey's choice of colors and designs reflect the client's love of country.

DIVINE DESIGN

Everyone at one time or another makes a decorating mistake. The lesson to be learned is: don't punish yourself and live with it, or worse, let it influence the rest of your decorating plans. Rather, take action right away and replace your mistake with what you now realize it should be. It might be a cliché, but life is too short to live with mistakes.

Kathy Dyer's dining room suggests country, with a touch of formality. The dark green traditional wallcovering mixes well with the country fabric.

This unique multi-layered asymmetric window treatment was just what the customer ordered!

DINING TRADITIONS

Navy and lavender were combined with classic Queen Anne furniture to create this formal dining room.

Faux (foh) is French for false, counterfeit. In decorating, the popular trend is faux finishes that look like marble, stone, or wood. This look is available in wallcovering, or can be painted on floors, walls or furniture. When done professionally, it is impossible to tell the real thing from the fake.

A unique layered window treatment sets this dining room apart from Sandra Perakis' neighbors. She had asked her Illinois decorator Pam Ernst for something different and asymmetric. Pam's ingenious solution was to combine a bold floral with a stripe and wrap them casually around a covered pole. The floral alone continues down one side of the window while two solids in shades of wisteria form a jabot and braided tieback. Semi-privacy was achieved with fan Roman shades. Deep rose faux-finish wallcovering provides a constant flattering glow.

The formal dining room, designed by Ohio decorator Bonnie Stadler for David and Diane Lohr, blends dark navy and lavender with a classic Queen Anne table and chairs. A pair of handsome diamond paned windows are treated to dressy swags and bishop sleeves. The table accessories and bordered area rug repeat the lush lavender.

SOFTENING WAY
WITH ANTIQUES

These two spacious dining rooms called for light and airy colors that would soften the antique furnishings. Florida decorators Carol Stearns and Tonya DeMaar were asked to work around the heavy mahogany pieces belonging to their client's mother.

Softly dramatic, a wide pink and white stripe paper covers the wall above the crisp white wainscoting. The new tiled floor provides a cool transition to the patio outside, while a floral area rug helps anchor the visual weight of the furniture. The simple sheer swag gracefully looped through corinthian brackets enhances the view without competing. Underneath are Duette shades for sun control. Carol Stearns and Tonya De Maar achieved an elegant balance between the heavy antique furniture and the new light colors and soft fabrics.

Cathy Buchanan's challenge for her Texas client was to create a design around the reproduction table and chairs, and an antique secretary/desk. Her fabric choice lightens the feeling of this charming room. The windows are treated to operable pencil-pleated cloud shades in a glorious bold stripe.

An elegant balance was achieved between the heavy antique furniture and the new light colors and soft fabrics.

Decorator Cathy Buchanan's fabric choices blend handsomely with the oriental style rug, while the colors lighten the feeling of the room.

KITCHENS

FROM A FASCINATING COUNTRY KITCHEN OUT OF DEVON, ENGLAND TO AN AWARD–WINNING OHIO MAKEOVER, FROM SMALL SPACES TO GENEROUS FLOOR PLANS, FROM NEWLY REMODELED ROOMS TO SIMPLY UPDATED ONES, THERE IS A WEALTH OF IDEAS ON THE FOLLOWING PAGES TO HELP YOU DESIGN YOUR DREAM KITCHEN. EACH EXAMPLE, WHETHER DESIGNED FOR A CLIENT OR THE DECORATOR HERSELF, SHOWS HOW FUNCTION AND COMFORT CAN BE INTEGRATED WITH INDIVIDUALITY AND BEAUTY.

AN AWARD
WINNING KITCHEN

All Decorating Den interior decorators will tell you that it is much easier to make decisions for clients than it is for themselves. Every week they are overwhelmed with new fabric samples, wallcovering books, and the latest home furnishing product information.

But the up side is that decorators can be more daring than most customers allow. "After dealing with a lot of clients who tend to be conservative, I wanted to design an eclectic room that would express my love for color," said 1993 Decorator of the Year Linda Lawson. Her own kitchen is a bold mixture of vibrant colors and interesting patterns.

Linda's red and white walls, green cabinets, accented with gold and white tile, and sharpened with slashes of black, fulfilled her need to be surrounded by color. By painting the existing cabinets Linda achieved an exciting new look, and at the same time was able to save money.

Old cabinets look new with a fresh coat of paint. The vibrant colors of this kitchen reflect Linda Lawson's sunny personality!

DIVINE DESIGN

If there is a Decorating Den trademark, it would have to be our knack for furnishing clients with money-saving ideas. The Decorating Den philosophy is to give clients great-looking rooms at the most affordable prices. This kitchen makeover by decorator Linda Lawson is a good example of what can be done with a little paint and a lot of imagination.

Linda is sentimental about her table which was given to her as a Mother's Day gift.

BRILLIANT BLANCHETTE

Linda Blanchette's collection of blue and white china is housed in "old pine" cabinets from Glasgow.

Linda Blanchette, Decorating Den international decorator, has achieved success in a relatively short time. A feature article in an English magazine said: "Linda's own home clearly demonstrates her talent for interior design." The Blanchettes live in the midst of rolling Devon Valley farmland in a converted 1850's granite barn with 18 inch rough-plastered walls and original ceiling beams.

The kitchen units are made of "old pine" from Glasgow, as is the table. The netting is galvanized chicken wire, a throwback to Linda's childhood in Kenya, where a similar mesh was used to keep out bugs and enable air to circulate around perishables. Linda's collection of mostly English and French blue and white china depicts various country scenes, with many of the plates dating back to the early 1700's. A lovely earthtone pomegranate print was used for curtains, shade and seat cushions. The sink is an old glazed "Butler" or "Belfast" sink. Linda tells us that her three cats are starting to make the new wicker chairs look "satisfactorily antique!" The multi-purpose AGA range, in sporty racing green, cooks the Blanchettes' food, heats their house, and provides them with hot water. Tiles above are from New Mexico.

An all-purpose AGA stove, new wicker chairs, and pine table define true English country style.

GREAT WHITE WAYS

In recent years white has resurfaced as a popular choice for remodeling old kitchens. Mother-and-daughter team, Sue Major of Pennsylvania and ASID Allied Member Julie Major Dabney of Virginia, were retained to add oomph to this kitchen, including cabinet selection and plans for enlarging the space. The Majors had a hard time convincing the client to use this dark wallcovering and border, although they knew it would visually improve the tall narrow look of the space with its nine foot ceilings and offer a dramatic contrast to all of the stark white. One of the trademarks of Decorating Den's decorators is listening. They answered his request for an updated look with a dramatic dark color that made his kitchen look fresh and new. In fact, he loved his kitchen makeover so much he married Julie the decorator!

Massachusetts ASID Allied Member decorator Robin Cotter was called in while this kitchen was being remodeled to select the wallcovering and window treatment, and place accessories, antiques and the client/watercolorist's art treasures. Robin chose the periwinkle pansy pattern for walls and valance and shade to make a crisp, cheerful presentation of these treasures.

The periwinkle pansy pattern gives the kitchen a crisp, light and cheerful feeling.

Dining chair seats were recovered in a coordinating print.

Dark wallpaper makes an enticing background for the new white cabinets.

CANADIAN PARADISO

Wall, floors, cabinets and furniture were kept simple. The room's panache comes from the spicy hot red accents, built-in eating nook, and one-of-a kind window treatments.

If you do not look beyond the shades, you would believe that this colorful sunny kitchen belonged in a tropical setting. Look a little closer. The view is a Canadian winter landscape. In addition, if you knew Decorating Den's Canadian decorator, Linda Baker, you would instantly recognize her happy and fanciful personality in this room. When she began redecorating, Linda said, "I want to create a truly unique area with room and inspiration for my active family to cook, entertain, draw, do homework, relax, and have fun." Low maintenance was also key, since Linda is very busy with her thriving decorating business. So her parrot collection set the direction for the exciting color scheme. Rather than compromise quality and look, Linda preferred to work on the project in stages, and keep to medium-priced products and fabrics.

Insulating shades are topped with hand-painted fabric valances that were done by a local artist.

Looking at Linda's bright and care-free decorating, you just know that this is a family that has fun together!

GOOD DESIGN

A glass table top adds to the light and airy feeling.

Aside from removing one of the ovens and replacing it with a microwave, it was not necessary to make any major structural changes to this well-designed kitchen. When it was first built, the kitchen won a design award and was featured in advertising by General Electric. Chicago interior decorator Dawn Wagner was called in to rejuvenate the dowdy kitchen. She brought new life into the room with a more fashionable color palette. Fresh peach was the choice for the ceramic floor and the countertops. The cabinets were repainted oyster white. An abstract sea foam floral print was used for the draperies, balloon valances, and to cover the seats of the new white rattan chairs.

Before, the floor plan was perfect, but that could not be said of the outmoded harvest gold and avocado green colors, which Dawn Wagner replaced when she rejuvenated this kitchen.

Peach flooring and countertops mixed with a seafoam print bring new life to this kitchen.

FIT FOR A GOURMET COOK

Oak furnishings combined with bright red guarantee a great start in this lively breakfast room.

Sherry Butterfield tailored plaid valences trimmed in blue over white blinds to dress the window.

Being a gourmet cook and always in the kitchen, Texas client Diane Hart dreamed of a beautifully designed space like those she had been envying in magazines. Sherry Butterfield, DDCD, Decorating Den's 1989 Decorator of the Year was given the happy task of fulfilling this client's delicious desire.

A bold red floral wallcovering makes an appetizing background for Diane's collection of blue and white plates. For a decorative as well as practical window treatment, Sherry designed tailored plaid valances trimmed in blue, over white wood blinds. Some of Diane's 360 cookbooks are on display.

THAT COUNTRY FEELING

Owner/decorator Carolyn Moore, DDCD, was dissatisfied with her tired looking kitchen. She wanted a complete remodeling job including new flooring, countertops, window treatments, wallcovering and paint. This project had been put on hold for several years because she wanted to do away with the cabinetry and start all over. Instead of waiting any longer, Carolyn decided to keep the existing cabinets, and just replace doors and drawer fronts.

Color inspiration for the newly madeover room comes from Moore's state flower, the Texas bluebonnet. This lovely medium blue tone combined with navy contrasts effectively with creamy white cabinets. Garage sale bookcases were given a fresh coat of paint, while a lattice cornice with a plant ledge was installed over the window. Playful arrangements of the Moore family treasures are exhibited throughout the kitchen.

A warm and welcoming place, especially for visiting grandchildren was the way the client described what she wanted to Michigan interior decorator Judith Roessler. Dark navy swag draperies mix with the light and airy wallcovering to provide a delightful background for the client's charming country accessories.

Navy swag draperies and the light and airy wallcovering give this kitchen breakfast area its charm, designed by Judith Roessler.

*Decorator Moore kept her cabinets
and just replaced the doors and drawer
fronts. Her country collectibles look
great in the new bright blue kitchen.*

A GEM OF A KITCHEN

Light oak cabinets, floors, and furnishings paved the way for this brilliant sapphire and white decorating scheme. The client asked Kathy Dyer, DDCD, an Ohio decorator, "to create an open and colorful contemporary kitchen around the newly tiled island and countertops."

Kathy, like all of her Decorating Den colleagues, saved her client hours of picking through hundreds of wallpaper books. In her sample- stocked Decorating Den ColorVan®, Kathy was able to find the perfect wallcovering. Working around the duo-tone blue tile samples, she happened upon a fabulous blue, lavender and teal contemporary floral design on a stark white background. This accented the tiled counters beautifully, and the coordinating border featured a black strip that tied in the glass kitchen appliances.

A crisp blue and white striped mock shade was used at the windows, and a new area rug with similar diagonal lines was placed under the table. These sparkling cool colors complement the warm wood tones.

Oak cabinets and duo-tone blue tiles
set the direction for for this striking
contemporary design.

FAMILY ROOMS

THIS MULTI-PURPOSE ROOM HAS MANY NAMES: MEDIA ROOM, STUDY, LIBRARY, GAME ROOM, DEN, AND MOST OFTEN FAMILY ROOM. THE NAMES MAY VARY, BUT THE ONE THING THESE ROOMS HAVE IN COMMON IS COMFORT. FURNITURE AND DECORATING STYLES WILL BE DIFFERENT, BUT THE MOOD IS SURE TO BE RELAXED AND INFORMAL. HERE IS THE IDEAL PLACE FOR A TOUCH OF WHIMSY, TRENDY THEMES, OR DISPLAYING FAMILY PHOTOS AND PERSONAL MEMENTOS UNTIL YOUR HEART'S CONTENT.

A PLAY ON PATTERN

A mix of patterns and designs, each one handsome in itself, can add tremendous éclat to a room. But it takes a person with a trained eye to be able to combine disparate motifs and make them all work together.

Ohio decorator Becky Shearn had the confidence to blend toile with check, flamestitch with animal symbols, exotic oriental rug design with rustic painted bench motifs, and in addition, toss in a wedding ring quilt. She used the same knack for mixing when it came to displaying her collection of antiques.

The treasured wicker furniture once white has been painted a delicious shade of apple red. White walls and floor provide a light and airy background for the warm color scheme. The simple, but striking window treatment adds a final gracious touch to the Shearn's cozy country family room.

Detail of window treatment with fabric-covered rod and informal swag.

The interesting window treatment and newly painted apple red wicker furniture mix well with Becky Shearn's delightful collection of patterns and antiques.

HAPPY MARRIAGE

Ruth Ann Fitzpatrick chose a glorious strawberry wall color as the perfect background for their wonderful collection of furnishings.

The gallery wall consists of artwork, including a few Jim Bugg originals, and objects accumulated mostly on trips to Decorating Den conferences.

The room began as just a family room, but became larger after the French doors were removed and the screened porch was converted to a sun room. Now year round they have the ideal spot to enjoy breakfast.

A classic dilemma in most households is how to reconcile the differing tastes of husbands and wives. When the wife is an interior decorator, the problem escalates. Ruth Ann Fitzpatrick ran into this predicament when she and her husband Michael began making plans to re-do their family room. "Michael leans toward contemporary and I am traditional," Ruth Ann explained. "So, our goal was to wed them into a look that we would both feel comfortable with."

There was a master plan and color scheme from the very beginning. But, rather than settle for less than what they really wanted, the Fitzpatricks allowed themselves a year to purchase the quality furnishings that they had their heart set on. As with Ruth Ann and Michael, the eclectic style and luscious colors of this room make a happy marriage.

MAKEOVER
FEATURED ON CBS

By moving the exercise equipment to the other side of the room, and the freshly skirted table and recovered chairs closer to the kitchen, the overall look of the room was greatly improved

"What can Decorating Den do, for a maximum of five thousand dollars, to bring a bright new life to this dark, rather dreary, wood paneled family room?" This question was posed to Maryland decorator Sharon Spring by the producers of CBS "This Morning." But clients Art Jaso and Sue Decker were opposed to the obvious solution of painting it. Sharon's personalized makeover was featured on national television on November 2, 1993.

The panelling remains, but now it acts as a frame around the updated window treatments. Sharon chose Waverly Southwest pastel prints because of Art's Mexican heritage. The four large windows are now hung with long side panels and tapered valances in one of the new fabrics. Hunter Douglas Duette shades provide privacy and sunlight. Sharon used a coordinating fabric to recover two armchairs and a durable blue textured fabric for the once tired beige sofa. A large mission style coffee table gives the Jasos a lot more space to display some of their new accessories. The rug they were saving for the living room turned out to be just perfect for this room.

Before the makeover

New accessories.

Southwest patterns and color palette give this once somber family room a refreshing update.

The heavy quality of the logs was relieved by lightweight wicker furniture and sunny fabrics.

COMFORT LIVES UP TO HER NAME

Susan Comfort's client Jan Gorecki, had purchased this Scandinavian style cottage located in Thunder Beach on Georgian Bay in Ontario,Canada, but two years later his family had still not moved in. Jan found the huge logs dark and overpowering, and when he tried to sell the house, prospective buyers had the same reaction.

That is when Jan told interior decorator Susan Comfort, "I want to redecorate from scratch!" Susan's main concern was how to relieve the heavy quality of the logs. Her first step was to replace, massive furnishings with light and airy wicker. The table and chairs given to the client by his daughter were retained, but refinished with a light oak stain.

One large Berber area rug, as well as the glass topped tables also add to the new open feeling. A Jacobean pattern with a soft sunshine yellow ground brightens the cushions and casual top treatment at the windows. When privacy is required vertical blinds that normally stack to the sides can be pulled across the windows.

The time frame for the completion was seven weeks. Now Jan has great reservations about selling his Comfort(able) decorated home!

COLLECTION INSPIRED

Both of these family rooms feature blue and have a masculine flavor, but each one reflects the individual personality of the homeowner.

Carol Stearns' and Tonya DeMaar's clients wanted to display a collection of antique nautical maps and sun motif objects. So they selected this deep blue green color accented in gold and sandy pink Mexican tile floor. Unattractive paneled walls are covered with a teal paper that helps show off the light maps. Large scaled upholstered pieces work well with iron leg tables with hatch-like wood tops. White pleated shades tuck underneath the paisley valance, allowing for the all-year-around Florida sunshine.

"Get rid of the country ducks!" Jan Tomlinson, DDCD, heard from Texas client Dale Ross, who asked her to tie his family room in with the Southwestern feeling of the adjacent rooms. Now for good listening and viewing there is a new leather upholstered sofa and Indian motif-covered chairs and ottoman. Walls and vaulted ceiling are sponge-painted a metallic blue, showcasing Dale's American Indian artifacts. The custom cornice complements an oak mantle, rescued from the attic and now displayed on the wall over the sofa.

A collection of American Indian artifacts set the tone for the Southwestern flavor of Dale Ross' den.

Nautical blues and sun motifs give this masculine family room its unique character.

*Hunter green fabrics and the new
cream color panelling are spiced with
paprika accents.*

The panelling remains unchanged, but vivid colors and fabrics bring new life to this family room.

TO PAINT OR NOT TO PAINT

One of the most difficult decisions when redecorating is whether or not to paint old wood panelling. Here is how two decorators solved the problem, using similar color schemes, but creating totally different atmospheres.

What spurred decorator Anne Fawcett's client Kathleen Moriarty to agree to painting her dark wood panelling? She had begun to redecorate her Massachusetts home, and after seeing how bright and cheery the other rooms looked, she knew that it was time to update her drab family room. Painting the dark wood walls a soft light cream was just the beginning of this major transformation. Beautiful wood floors were exposed after the old wall to wall carpet was removed. Exquisite area rugs now define cozy areas, and visually break the long narrow expanse of the room

In the case of Canadian decorator Joan Watchorn and her client Marie Clarke, the decision was to revitalize the existing panelling by sanding and revarnishing. The lively vivid colors in the contemporary fabrics of the draperies and sofa brighten the look of this delightful Northern family room.

An existing closet that protrudes into the room has become a work of art. Kathleen's beautiful black dog Barnaby is the focal point of a trompe l'oeil mural.

DIVINE DESIGN

Take a leaf from ASID Allied Member and DDCD interior decorator Anne Fawcett's idea book...don't hesitate to brighten up your dreary old panelling. The choices are numerous... paint, wallcovering, antiquing, fabric, a scenic mural...or use your imagination!

TURNING A "WRECK" INTO A REC ROOM

Adults also enjoy this transformed dreary basement rec room.

Maintaining the casual, easy-care theme are a built-in banquette, directors chairs, and a twig table. Inexpensive baskets dot the walls.

This Connecticut interior decorator did a masterful job of converting a dreary basement into an attractive and carefree family room. Eileen Holden was asked to make a rec room out of an existing "wreck." Because of the double challenge of possible water damage and heavy use by teenagers, it was necessary to select practical and low maintenance materials and flooring. But, at the same time the client wanted the basement room to have a happy and inviting atmosphere.

Perennial color favorite mauve was combined with crisp white and watery blues for a happy result. A commercial grade carpet made for wearability and water resistance is one of the practical selections. Spot resistant Indian print fabrics merged with indestructible furnishings such as the built-in cabinets and converted spool table keep the room worry free.

A collection of multi-colored masks decorate one of the walls.

LIGHT AND LOVELY

These two rooms have come a long way from their "shady" pasts. Both clients were looking for a "light-lift" for their much-used family rooms.

Sharon Knox's client's room got a total remodeling: a new furniture arrangement makes it easy to watch T.V. (enclosed in the cabinet), take in the beautiful California view, or gaze at the gorgeous stone fireplace. A freshly painted white ceiling and mirror add to the bright new feeling.

Soft colors, a plump sectional sofa and light pine furniture gave April Harrison's clients a comfortable room for everyday living, but equally inviting for casual entertaining. Colors from the rest of the house are echoed in the luscious fabric. With a variety of green plants, April adds a perennial spring-like feeling to this pleasant Ohio house.

Left, a luscious plaid sectional sofa and pine furniture suit the casual entertaining style of this family.

Right, planned for comfort and easy viewing of the outdoors, the fireplace, or the television (enclosed in the cabinet).

GARDEN VISIONS

Beautiful florals combine with plaids to create a formal country mood.

Dreading the dismal winter months, these Northern homeowners dreamed of having a room that would feel like a summer garden all year around. In addition, they wanted a gracious place for holiday entertaining and family gatherings.

This spacious family room was once a small third bedroom. Illinois decorator Lynnay Kallemeyn's idea of extending the room up as well as out added drama and excitement to what otherwise might have been merely another space. Beautiful florals come together with plaids to create a formal country mood. A local artist painted the trailing ivy on the walls and some of the pieces of furniture.

Interior decorator Mary Ann Reilly answered her Pennsylvania client's love for red and green when she found this pair of voluptuous prints. Natural wicker furniture is covered in bountiful bouquets of red flowers and lush green foliage, while rod pocket bell style valances are made out of the striking plaid panel stripe. As daylight falls, pleated shades hidden behind the valances can be pulled down for privacy and warmth. A rouge tinted strié wallcovering bestows a constant warm glow on the room.

Natural wicker and lush floral prints give this Northern family room a garden glow all year long.

EVERYDAY IS "SUN" DAY

This family room belongs to Georgia interior decorator Terri Ervin. Originally it was a screened-in porch that she described as, "a large dog house for her three dogs." From the time Terri moved into her lovely old farmhouse, she had visions of converting this space, with its secluded woodland view, into a wonderful sunroom.

A brilliant floral chintz frames the new windows. Cushy buttery yellow-striped loveseats mated with wicker and rattan, and a charming ottoman coffee table create a soft, but sophisticated feeling.

A pass through to kitchen.

In the corner, a white lace bordered cloth covers the green and white skirted table. Needlepoint pillows mix with plaid and floral ones.

This inviting room blends sunshine colors and green wicker with brilliant florals and stripes.

Mary Perritt's selection of a billiard green wallcovering sets the right tone for this lively pool room. Note the detail around the framed prints.

FUN AND GAMES

Here are three rooms decorated for fun and games. Michigan decorator Carol Sanborn created a relaxed atmosphere compatible with frequent family entertaining and the activities of three teenagers. Because of the proximity to the main rooms of the house, Mary Perritt's Georgia clients needed their pool room to look great all of the time. In Texas, Beverly Baldwin was asked by her clients to convert a former spare bedroom into a cozy, comfortable "old English billiard parlor."

Deep rich colors add warmth and contrast to the neutral background in this family room decorated by Carol Sanborn.

A unique border surrounds this all purpose billiard parlor. The "club" atmosphere created by Beverly Baldwin attracts the entire family to this once spare bedroom.

VARIATIONS ON A GLOBAL THEME

These two multi-purpose rooms perform a trio of duties. Often they are places where family and friends gather, other times they might play host to an overnight guest, and frequently they become quiet studies for reading and working.

Tulsa antique dealer Sam Spacek's own home represents his business well. Decorator Jan Chilcoat helped Sam and his wife Malissa develop a fitting background to showcase their select assortment of European antiques. Walls are treated to a combination of library paper, burnished and burgundy wallcoverings, and a border featuring a series of globes. Legs were cut off the 17th century French farm table that now serves as a generous coffee table. Plaid, leather, and dark rich colors continue the worldly ambience of the Spacek's study.

Warm coppery tones mixed with forest greens, and plaid combined with an earthy tree-of-life print, are a few of the ingredients that make this room a feast for the eyes. Alan Patricio had asked Georgia interior decorator Judith Slaughter to turn his tiny (10 foot X 14 foot) "catchall" space into a room suitable for entertaining, for putting up overnight guests, and to be his home office. With bamboo-styled furniture and tailored window treatments Judith created the epitomé of a refined gentleman's study.

Built-in bookshelves and cabinets provide adaptable work space.

One corner of the room, right, is devoted to their collection of unique clocks.

*Copper tones and forest greens
combined with an earthy print make
this room, left, a feast for the eyes.*

*Plaid, leather and dark rich colors are
a fitting background for Sam Spacek's
antiques.*

COSMOPOLITAN COUNTRY

Custom wood furniture, sisal carpet, damask draperies and an eclectic collection of art give this sitting room its cosmopolitan flavor.

England's Devon Valley is the beautiful setting of interior decorator Linda Blanchette's restored mid-nineteenth century barn. In her handsomely decorated second floor sitting room one is keenly aware of her childhood in Kenya and interest in worldwide design. Linda's blending of Turkish rugs, Navaho and Suni pots, African artifacts, French paintings, mixed with those of local artists, created a very personal room with a true cosmopolitan flavor.

Furniture determined the decoration. The sideboard, coffee table, china cabinet were made from a sycamore tree with unusual rippling through it, by a well-known North Devon designer, David Savage. A pair of "Camelot" chairs are made out of pear wood. Flooring is sisal, richly contrasted with damask curtains. The braid trim on the curtains picks up colors of the sofas and the Donald Hamilton Fraser seascapes.

The 18 inch thick walls are rough plaster and painted, and the beams are all original oak. Local stone and slate were used to construct the fireplace. Rugs are antique Turkish Herehkes. On a holiday in France, the Blanchettes found the large Grahame Bannister oil painting.

The fireplace is made of local stone and slate, the rugs are from Turkey, and the large oil painting is from France.

SYBARITIC SPA

The ancient Greeks of Sybaris, noted for their love of luxury and pleasure, have nothing on the Hones of Ohio. The bubbling hot tub was in place when interior decorator DeDe Layer was called in to design a luxurious setting for the Hone's family room.

An all-year-around vacation atmosphere was produced with comfortable wicker furniture, lots of cool clean white complemented by tropical colors and patterns. Light filtering, yet private, Hunter Douglas Silhouette shades are topped with bright soft valances that match the draw draperies over the sliding glass door.

A hot tub in a tropical setting is the perfect place to relax and unwind after a stressful day.

MASTER BEDROOMS

SOMETIMES WE FORGET HOW MUCH TIME WE REALLY SPEND IN OUR MASTER BEDROOMS. READING THROUGH SEVERAL THOUSAND ENTRIES, WHEN DECORATING DEN JOINED WITH WOMAN'S DAY MAGAZINE IN SPONSORING A DREAM BEDROOM CONTEST, REINFORCED MY BELIEF THAT EVERYONE NEEDS A SOOTHING, BEAUTIFUL, AND PERSONAL BEDROOM. IT WAS REASSURING TO LEARN THAT SO MANY COUPLES HAD GOOD MARRIAGES, AND FELT THAT HAVING A ROMANTIC HIDEAWAY FOR THEMSELVES WOULD PERPETUATE THEIR LOVING FEELINGS. THE MASTER BEDROOM SEEMS TO BE THE LAST ROOM THAT EVERYONE DECORATES, AND YET CONSIDERING THE AMOUNT OF TIME WE SPEND THERE, IT SHOULD BE THE FIRST.

WOMAN'S DAY
DREAM WINNERS

Decorating Den joined with *Woman's Day* magazine in sponsoring a Dream Bedroom Contest. We received thousands of entries from all across America, each one expressing a desire for a master bedroom that would be a romantic escape. I hope these winning makeovers will be an inspiration for everyone to stop waiting and do something about having a dream bedroom NOW!

Decorators Shirley Rosenberg and Robyn McNelly were given the responsibility of designing this recent master bedroom addition for Judy and Richard Deatherage of California. Shirley described the room, "It was bright and spacious, but lacked the variety that comes from the use of texture, color, and fabric."

The Deatherages' favorite colors, deep red and navy were brought into play with the fabric selected for the luxurious reversible comforter. A soft, airy linen casually envelops the new four poster bed which fits in handsomely with the Deatherages' antiques. The subtle beige and white stripe of the dust ruffle is echoed on the walls. Shutters and personal accessories complete the dreamy picture.

* Dark red and navy play off of subtle beige and white for the dreamy makeover of the first place master bedroom winners.

Prizewinners Diane and Erin Lantry of Indiana had been stumped with how to decorate their long narrow bedroom with its sloping ceiling, but it was just another challenge for experienced interior decorators JoAnne North and Debbie Staples. Rearranging the furniture was the first step. Placing the bed on a long low wall freed up space for a wicker settee in one corner, and a television/storage cabinet in the other.

Walls were given a custom paint job by sponging two shades of pink over white, and stenciling ivy over new built-in drawers. The soft colors of the floral chintz, the lovely vanity, and the fresh white wicker combined with the quilt made by Diane's mother, make this the romantic room the Lantrys had always dreamed about.

Serene seafoam green and rose were the color directions suggested by Anne Fawcett and Debby Day when they were asked to decorate Massachusetts winner Ginny Falkoff's bedroom. It was to be a major change from the previous purple-toned room. Ginny's delicate headboard and other furniture also underwent a color change with white paint and pastel highlights for the carvings. A beautiful pattern of luscious floral stripes graces the bed and repeats in the balloon shades. A new area rug was the final touch.

Seafoam green and rose turned this once purple bedroom into a soothing oasis for the third place winners.

*The second place winners were
treated to soft new colors, sponged and
stenciled walls, and floral chintz.

THE MORE THE MERRIER

Decorator Sharon Henson rewarded
herself with this beautifully appointed
traditional master suite. Evergreen
accents add a rich contrast to the light
and airy room.

*If you want to feel more comfortable
about mixing different patterns, and
have a desire to be bolder when it
comes to combining colors, look to
the world of art. By studying
painters who were exceptionally
masterful at juxtaposing a variety
of designs with a wealth of color,
you will open your eyes to the realm
of combination possibilities. The
brilliant paintings of Vuillard,
Bonnard, and Matisse encourage
the viewer to be more passionate
about, and experimental with
mixing colors and patterns.
Professional decorators like Linda
Yates and Sharon Henson are there
to educate and encourage those
clients who want this unique and
individual look.*

The braid trim on the comforter and
the shirred fabric with gimp trim on
the lampshades are two of the elegant
custom touches that blend patterns in
exuberant colors in this warm and
lovely bedroom.

Most people have a fear of mixing more than two patterns, but
not these two decorators.

Michigan decorator Linda Yates' masterful blending of prints
is heightened by her exuberant choice of colors. The predomi-
nant pattern, plaid, is coordinated with a solid fabric to create
an adventurous mix. Light background floral bouquets for the
walls and bed accents are further enhanced by touches of a
leafy bargello, a stripe, and a mini flower print. Linda said, "My
client, Kimberly Porembiak, appreciates detail in her decorating, and her master bedroom reflects this."

Texas interior decorator Sharon Henson designed this
romantic retreat for the pleasure of her husband and herself. A
mirrored wall reflects their traditional furniture, cherished
accessories, and a wonderful array of textures and patterns. An
unusual pleated headboard was one of Sharon's custom details.

Earthy colors, plump bedding and
plantation shutters give this room its
Old World/new life aura.

WHAT A WAY TO RETIRE!

The beauty of the gold damask Indian cotton sheets was enhanced with rich tapestry and a voluptuous window treatment.

By the time the Moore's retired, Jean Moore knew exactly how she wanted to furnish and decorate their new house. For years Jean dreamed of retiring...retiring to a beautifully decorated bedroom that is! She asked Texas decorator Bonnie Pressley, DDCD, to help make her dreams of a warm, beautiful, and lightly romantic bedroom become a reality. The color scheme is an earthy mixture of salmon, adobe, blush, cedar and sage. Plump headboards, outline quilted spreads, soft swag and plantation shutters create an Old World/new life aura for this serenely elegant retreat.

The color scheme that Ohio decorator Kathy Dyer, DDCD, selected is meant to complement her client Diane Bryant's fabulous set of gold damask Indian cotton sheets. A rich multi-colored tapestry throw spread with a velvet turnback, and masses of luxurious pillows give the bed an ultra-rich look. The voluptuous window treatment is given a neoclassic twist with the addition of a green damask swag panel, trimmed in gold piano fringe. These elegant fabrics are repeated on the skirted table.

FOUR POSTERS

The four poster bed is ever-popular and always romantic—in a brand new house or an ancient one. In these examples, from Texas to Virginia, our Decorating Den decorators have used the four poster as the master bedroom's focal point, but each is decked our to reflect the client's style and budget.

An elegant play of color and pattern completely revitalized the once drab room in a modern-day house deep in the heart of Texas. Decorator Sandra Scott describes her treatment for the rice bed, "The bed envelops you with its suspended cornice of a hovering lace butterfly cascade."

This gracious master bedroom is in keeping with traditional Virginia style. Using the lovely cherry four poster bed as the focal point, decorators Barbara Ginman and Virginia Miller created a genteel ambience that pleases both husband and wife. Bed and window treatments are soft but tailored, and feminine pinks are mixed with more masculine navies.

Connecticut decorator Eileen Holden designed a glorious haven for a busy career couple. Both have stressful jobs and wanted a restful retreat to come home to. Their beautiful mahogany furniture has been enhanced with an array of English country chintzes. The canopy and bed treatment add to the importance of the handsome four poster.

Long after her long stemmed roses fade interior decorator Terri Ann Parks and her husband Bruce will still be surrounded by lush rose walls and the beautiful floral chintz she chose for their own bedroom. A striking red and white stripe adds to the charm of the bed and the window.

SOUTHWEST ORIGINAL

Clients often ask for something different, but are not always willing to go out on a limb. Texas decorator Becky Aleman knew when she met C. Delle Bates that he was very open to new ideas. An avid art collector and an artist himself, C. Delle wanted lots of color and a Southwest look for his bedroom.

Dark navy wallcovering provides the ideal backdrop for showing off the strong colors of paintings and fabrics. A dramatic four poster bed was custom-built in Santa Fe, and is definitely the center of attention in this small room. Other eyecatchers are the unique lamps.

One of C. Delle's treasured pieces is the area rug that came from former Texas Governor John Connally's home. A subtle final touch to this original room is the sophisticated paisley border and matching fabric.

The dramatic four poster is the center of attention in this colorful Southwest bedroom.

CONTEMPORARY COMPLEMENTS

Giant irises airbrushed on the bedspread and window treatment make this room a romantic sensation.

It used to be just a long narrow space with high ceilings. Now this master suite is a romantic sensation. The soft color palette was inspired by the painting of the California coast. Decorator Marilyn Gill explains the room, "The use of giant iris, two tub chairs, and a round ottoman satisfied both the need for simplicity and curves. Twenty feet of vertical blinds and cornice were air-brushed, as well as the fabric for bedspread and headboard."

Originally Lois Pade's client had planned on using a pastel color scheme to match her carpet. When Lois saw the wood ceiling and the generous size of the room, she recommended this bolder, deeper color palette. Two lounge chairs and a striking new table create a cozy corner. Cornices and vertical blinds cover corner patio doors. These contemporary decorating elements suit the architectural style of this Wisconsin home.

Decorator Lois Pade, DDCD, steered her client in the right direction with this rich deep color palette.

MIRACLES DO HAPPEN

Same spaces, same windows, same furniture, but definitely not the same bedrooms! These are the kinds of transformations that Decorating Den is known for.

"Give me a beautiful room, not overly feminine, but definitely romantic," asked Marilyn Strassel of Ohio interior decorator, Debra Rose — a simple request with many challenges! Odd angles prevented moving the bed from beneath the off-centered window, so she hid it behind a dramatic backdrop. The walls are covered with a peach faux finish paper.

Similar problems faced another Ohio decorator, Diana Apgar. First a heat duct had to be moved so the bed could be centered on a different wall. Then lush floral patterns in the client Susan Evers' favorite rose color were used for banded, tapered valances and draperies to frame shuttered windows, for plumb ruffled pillow shams, and for the exquisite custom coverlet. Generous skirted tables hold a pair of lovely alabaster lamps and treasured family moments. Diana gave her client a dream room she hates to leave, and is proud to see published!

The platform bed has been cleverly disguised with a sumptuous padded headboard and plush bedcoverings.

Before

*Lush floral patterns in the client's
favorite rose color made this room "...so
beautiful she never wants to leave it."*

Before

HEAVENLY HAVENS

Yards and yards of fabric create a royal enclosure around the bed and windows.

The romantic feeling of these two fabulous bedrooms is the result of a dynamic collaboration between client and decorator. You'd have to travel far and wide to find bedrooms more inviting than these.

Jan Kuethe's clients the Wessons did not care to leave Texas to enjoy a beautiful getaway retreat. They desired to come home to one every night! Jan designed a beautiful room that is both formal and elegant, yet warm and cozy at the same time.

Carol and Tonya's lofty swag design in a lovely pink floral chintz is installed over Silhouettes shades in the new bathroom.

A serene and elegant master suite was designed for the Ruckels by two Florida decorators, Carol Stearns and Tonya DeMaar. Walls were painted a flattering rose beige. The suite's new bathroom design incorporates a glass block shower, jacuzzi tub, white cabinets, and dark green marble floor.

A serene bedroom was achieved with flattering rose beige walls, silvery tone-on-tone chintz, and a gorgeous window treatment.

SLEEPING IN A 17TH CENTURY COTTAGE

Lack of architectural detail and charm in many American homes add immeasurably to the job of the interior decorator. That was hardly the case when British decorator Rita Aston was asked to help renovate Mr. and Mrs. Duxbury's lovely 17th century thatched cottage. The problem was rebuilding after a major fire had swept through their house. Rita, and the ease of working with Decorating Den, simplified the restoration process and added a refreshing new look to the Duxbury's cottage.

One of the rooms to receive a major facelift was their master bedroom. Originally done in pinks, the Duxburys wanted a new brighter color scheme. The yellow rag-roll effect wallpaper sets a sunny new tone for the room. Draping the window and covering the pine bed in a lush blue and yellow Spanish-style print gave the room additional warmth.

A small eyebrow window over the bed is treated to a frilled valance, while the gable window has pencil pleat curtains, topped by a short valance. To further accent the V-shaped gable, Rita designed a throw swag that is kept in place with button holdbacks. Deep blue chintz adds a striking color contrast.

The rebirth of the rustic charm of the Duxbury's cottage is complemented by Rita Aston's new uplifting decorating scheme.

THE DECORATOR'S DETAILS

Decorators are dreamers, too. When interior decorator Terri Ervin finally got around to designing a bedroom for herself and her husband Allen Hugo, she rolled out the very best of her decorating talent. For the previous homeowners, this was a child's room. Now looking at the room's new appearance and Terri's extraordinary attention to detail, it is hard to believe that her goal was to fix it up as inexpensively as possible.

Terri combined soft seafoam with vibrant reds to create a warm and inviting retreat. Walls were papered in a delicate stripe over the existing covering. Crown molding and border were added, as well as the new ceiling fan lights. Graceful floral

Graceful floral and lace swags, caught with fabric rosettes, romantically frame the windows and canopy the bed.

and lace swags, caught with fabric rosettes, romantically frame the windows and canopy the bed.

The skirted night table is topped with a glorious plaid that picks up all the colors of the main print. A couple of clocks from Terri's extensive collection, a variety of ruffled shams and needlepoint pillows, gold framed botanical prints, and a tassel accent for her crystal lamp...are all fine examples of Terri's eye for style and design.

A sample of Terri's attention to detail.

*The plaid skirted night table holds
some of Terri's treasures.*

BEAUTIFUL BEDS

The sensuous seafoam walls provide a beautiful backdrop for an antique Victorian bed dressed in vintage linens and lace decorated by Meyers, Eten and Wells.

A charming array of pretty prints make this a happy room designed by Paula Wells.

Delicate blue-green is the color for this soothing master bedroom suite. California decorator Barbara Addicott was asked by the Hardys, her career couple clients, to create a restful retreat around their love for antiques. Soft hues and gentle patterns create a harmonious atmosphere for the lovely furnishings. Upholstered traverse rods work well over French doors that open inward.

The delighted townhouse owner describes the new bedroom, "It is such a happy room to wake up in!" Paula Wells, an interior decorator from Kentucky coordinated the charming array of pretty burgundy accented blue and white prints. Duette shades filled the bill when it came to privacy.

Three Kentucky decorators, Cheri Meyers, Kathy Eten and Paula Wells worked together on this romantic bedroom. The sensuous seafoam walls provide a beautiful backdrop for an antique Victorian bed dressed in vintage linens and lace. Muted floral bed throw and pillow shams coordinate with the delicate wallcovering and border.

Soft hues and gentle patterns create a harmonious atmosphere for the lovely furnishings, designed by Barbara Addicott.

A special custom addition is the exquisite Russian hand-knotted rug made to match the fabric in this master bedroom suite.

DELICIOUS CANOPIES

For a dramatic bed setting there is nothing quite like the allure of a canopy. Here are three adaptations of the style; classic traditional, cozy country, and exotic Oriental.

Illinois decorator Pam Ernst gave her clients exactly what they asked for...a formal, elegant and unique master bedroom. The imposing cherry four poster bed was made even more impressive with the addition of the canopy and stunning valance. Indigo and burgundy, mixed with champagne is an appropriately handsome color scheme.

One look at this bedroom and you can not help but feel warm and safe from modern day stresses. Indiana decorator Margaret Waddell used a country check with a mini floral print to create a cozy nostalgic atmosphere around her client's antique bed.

The ebony bed makes a strong focal point in this Oriental flavored room. North Carolina decorator Lynn Nacewicz, DDCD, continued the style with shaped cornices, ginger jar lamps, and wall accessories. The light coral and celadon gives the room an interesting color contrast.

The Oriental inspired ebony furniture was given a coral and celadon fabric contrast.

Country checks combined with a mini floral create a cozy nostalgic atmosphere.

The imposing four poster bed was made even more impressive with the addition of a stunning canopy.

BATHROOMS

LUXURY SEEMS TO BE THE OPERATIVE WORD WHEN IT COMES TO DECORATING TODAY'S BATHROOMS. THERE IS NOTHING QUITE LIKE SINKING INTO A SUMPTUOUS TUB IN A BEAUTI-FULLY DECORATED ROOM TO REJUVENATE ONE'S BODY AND SPIRIT. BUT DESIGNING A NEW BATHROOM OR REMODELING AN OLD ONE CAN BE A MAJOR CHALLENGE. NOT ONLY DO YOU HAVE TO SELECT A MULTITUDE OF PRODUCTS FROM AN OVER-WHELMING NUMBER OF CHOICES, BUT WITH THE EXCEPTION OF THE WALLCOVERING AND TOWELS, YOUR CHOICES WILL BE PERMANENT FIXTURES. ENLISTING PROFESSIONAL ADVICE WILL SAVE YOU MONEY, AND MANY HOURS OF GRIEF.

STRIPE UP THE BATH!

Edie Stull, DDCD, had a client who loved her new home's master bath, but hated the intense purple wallpaper chosen by the previous owner. Although the window required privacy, the client requested it be kept light and open. Edie made it her goal to integrate the striking architectural features and hand painted tiles, with her client's love for romantic Victorian accessories.

Focus was achieved by using simple, yet classic, striped wallpaper highlighting the Palladian window. A soft valance in an impressionistic floral enhances the romantic mood. Privacy is quick and convenient with the drop of a pleated shade.

Before

A classic striped wallcovering sets a dramatic background for the luxurious tub and Palladian window.

TRANQUIL HARMONY

The client's wish for simple window treatments called for Duette shades.

Cool surfaces and sleek lines are softened by the subtle pattern of the traditional wallpaper.

Robin Cotter's client had just undergone a total renovation of his Massachusetts oceanside home. He had gutted a small bedroom to make a masterbath with cathedral ceilings. Starting from scratch, Robin helped in making all of the major selections.

Although her client prefers contemporary architecture, his taste overall is somewhat eclectic. Cool surfaces and sleek lines are softened by the subtle pattern of the traditional wallpaper, while one choice piece of the client's Japanese art brings a touch of color to the monochromatic scheme.

Duette shades fulfill the client's wish for simple window treatments. All in all the bathroom emits a tranquil harmony associated with Oriental design.

UPDATED VERSIONS

Becky Shearn gave her own half bath a new ambience with a trompe l'oeil library wallpaper. She resurrected a family heirloom antique sink to replace the former humdrum vanity. An antique mirror, various collectibles, and the inexpensively framed prints of places the Shearns have visited in Germany give the room its unique personality.

Bathroom fixtures were kept intact, but Patti Peyer and Barbara Young, two California decorators spruced up a tired looking room with bright new wallcoverings and border. The original clear glass skylight was embellished with a custom designed stained glass overlay.

Bright new wallcoverings and border spruced up this California bathroom.

This bath was given an intriguing new ambience with trompe l'oeil library wallpaper.

IRRESISTIBLE BATHS

Before decorating brought things into perspective, this bathroom addition to a log home had an almost cavernous feeling. One of interior decorator Patricia Lahr's suggestions for visually altering the space was to add the horizontal line of lighting above the cabinets. Another was to use large accessories to keep everything in scale with the high ceiling. A soft vine design wallcovering effectively contrasts with the dark wood tones and river blue carpet.

Dramatic pattern and color changes surround the sumptuous jacuzzi bath, decorated by Bonnie Stadler. Cool white tile mixes with warm wood, while a light wallcovering is interestingly juxtaposed next to a dark design.

The light wallcovering offers a pleasing contrast to the dark wood tones and river blue carpet.

Two contrasting wallcoverings add an interesting touch to the sumptuous jacuzzi bath.

GOLF ENTHUSIASTS

In golf terms, this bathroom is a hole in one!

No need to ask what the Meyer's favorite sport is! Being avid golfers and living in a condominium overlooking a golf course, they requested that theme for the bath off of their family room. Inspiration bound, Kentucky decorator Kathy Eten devised a one of a kind design.

Old-fashioned ladies and gentlemen in knickers, or plus fours (depending on which country you happen to be in while reading this) are getting ready to tee off in a fanciful wallpaper border. The mini plaid shower curtain is accented with a unique topper to imitate flags from the first and eighteenth holes. Many interesting accessories complete the look, including a golf club towel rack that can easily be removed on the rare occasion this shower is used by guests.

GUEST ROOMS

A BEAUTIFUL ARRAY OF INVITING GUEST ROOMS IS ABOUT TO
UNFOLD BEFORE YOUR EYES. THOUGH THESE ROOMS OFTEN
SERVE MULTIPLE PURPOSES, THE DECORATORS AND THEIR
CLIENTS GAVE FIRST CONSIDERATION TO CREATING LOVELY,
COMFORTABLE, AND RESTFUL PLACES FOR THEIR GUESTS. AFTER
A NIGHT IN ANY ONE OF THESE ROOMS, EVEN THE MOST WEARIED
VISITOR WOULD FEEL REFRESHED AND AT HOME.

SERENE AND SOOTHING

A guest room often makes the bottom of the priority list when it comes to budgeting home decorating projects. Add to that the assumption that it has to cost a lot of money to be a beautifully decorated room. This was not the case when it came to Jessie Yao working with decorator Joan Suzio to create an inviting room for her guests.

The decision was made to put the emphasis on wonderful fabrics, and a built-in window seat with cedar storage space. Joan selected unfinished furniture which was painted white and then embellished with designs echoing the flowers in the fabric. Jessie Yao plans ultimately to hand down this furniture to her first granddaughter. Instead of wallcovering, the walls were painted a tranquil green and finished with a paper border. Soothing green and rosy pinks carry out the color scheme set by the rest of the gracious Illinois home.

Before the charming changes were made.

Tranquil green and rosy pinks set the soothing tone for this lovely guest room.

BEGUILING PERSONALITIES

Many collectors are unsure of how best to display their finds. Texas interior decorator Jan Tomlinson, DDCD, is an old hand at accessorizing, and had a lot of fun arranging her treasures in her newly decorated guest room. A gorgeous fabric of bountiful floral stripes layered on black, one of Jan's favorite colors created a sophisticated country atmosphere. Faux marbleized walls are contrasted with white trim and crown molding. A polished brass rod, antique lace, and a shade of black and white stripes make a striking backdrop for the angled family heirloom bed. Jan lined a white shelf with small rustic chairs, and hung her groupings of framed 1920's sayings on the walls.

Waking up to the warm Florida sunshine in this beguiling room has prolonged many a visitor's stay. A little used corner bedroom has been beautifully adapted by Carol Stearns and Tonya DeMaar into a lovely guest room. Fresh white wicker furnishings and a "sweet violet" print are perfect companions. Practical pleated shades are easily adjustable for light and privacy.

Fresh white wicker and a violet print prove to be the perfect companions for this Florida guest room. Sprigs of ivy, gathered from the fabric design embellish the corner walls.

A sophisticated country atmosphere was created with gorgeous florals and stripes against faux marbleized walls. Country collectibles complete this interesting guest room.

ROOMS AWAY FROM HOME

Bestowing not only a turn-of-the-century feeling on her guest room, but the ambience of a Victorian child's bedroom, was the wish of Georgia decorator, Rebecca Avery's client. A soft willow green moire and the plentiful mixture of patterns provides a charming background for her abundant collection of treasures. A melange of hooked and crocheted rugs distracts the eye from the aging carpet underneath. Related accessories are clustered together for added importance.

Because this room is small and seldom used, decorator Faith Sears was asked to work within a limited budget. Her first suggestion was to move the bed into the corner to make the room seem less cramped. Billowy sheer fabric dressed with trailing ivy for the window, and the crisp white painted walls, also add to a new more spacious feeling. Red accents on a bold green and white floral stripe give a bit of punch to this restful room away from home.

Billowy sheers, trailing ivy, and angling the bed in the corner add to the room's spacious feeling.

A soft green moire and a mixture of patterns provide a charming background for an abundant collection of treasures.

A DIVINE DUO

*A cherished canopy bed and flattering
pink hues beckon guests to this divine
room.*

The Marshalls are the third generation to occupy their splendid twenty-two room Delaware home. They asked interior decorator Julia Hughes to revive the guest room, not redecorated for 70 years. Using her client's vintage furniture and soft blue and rose fabrics and wallcovering from The First Lady Collection, Julia brought the room back to its original Victorian graciousness.

Georgia interior decorator Terri Ervin's guest room is full of sentimental attachments, but none more cherished than the beautiful canopy bed that Terri's father, Dr. John W. Ervin, had made for his daughter's sixteenth birthday. Terri has thought of everything down to choosing a luscious shade of pink to flatter her lucky visitors — including my husband and me — who remember with great pleasure the divine time spent in Terri's unabashedly feminine and romantic guest room.

*Soft blue and rose fabrics and
wallpaper brought this room back to
its original graciousness.*

CHILDREN'S ROOMS

FROM THE EARLIEST STAGES OF LIFE IT IS IMPORTANT THAT CHILDREN BE EXPOSED TO BEAUTY, COLOR, AND DESIGN. WHAT BETTER PLACE TO START THAN IN THE HOME, AND NO BETTER ROOM THAN A CHILD'S OWN SPACE. EXPERTS IN CHILD DEVELOPMENT WILL TELL YOU THAT GROWING UP IN PLEASANT SURROUNDINGS NURTURES A HEALTHY PRIDE. THE CHILDREN, WHOSE ROOMS ARE FEATURED IN THIS CHAPTER, HAVE BEEN GIVEN VISUALLY STIMULATING HEADSTARTS ON LEARNING TO APPRECIATE BEAUTY AND GOOD DESIGN, AS WELL AS FEELING GOOD ABOUT THEMSELVES.

*The doorway through the tree trunk is
the boys' entrance into their own private
playing space.*

MATT AND ZACH

The two lively young brothers, Matt and Zach, whose bedrooms are seen here, share the amusing playroom shown on the previous page. Another thing they have in common is the baseball team they both root for, the Atlanta Braves. Decorator/mom Terri Ervin Hugo hired an artist to paint the fantasy mural for her sons' attic playroom.

Matthew's durable yet attractive room was decorated for a boy who loves sports and the color blue. Red plaid and royal blue were the pick for a prince of a son.

The metal locker opens to reveal an 8 by 8 foot secret hiding and playing place.

Mom chose a star wallpaper and sports border for her sports star son Zach. Masculine colors and patterns that won't show dirt and grime were the practical choices for this room.

"GRAND" DAUGHTERS

An unfinished chest becomes a work of art in Jacqueline's room.

Jacqueline is bound to grow up with a flair for decorating. Georgia DDCD interior decorator Judith Slaughter and Jacqueline's grandmother designed a very colorful and imaginative room. Using bright pastels, Judith developed an "indoor-outdoor" theme with tulip borders, awning, and wicker furniture. An artist painted the delightful trompe l'oeil window, and Jacqueline's other grandmother made the quilt. The bed was an idea Judith stole from a movie, and Daddy built for her. Rather than putting the prominent border at the ceiling, Judith installed it closer to her grandchild's eye level.

Susan Comfort's client asked her to create a dream room for his "grand" daughters to stay in when they visited at his Canadian cottage. The room is furnished with twin Muskoka pine beds and an antique wicker chair. Pink candy striped cotton, Battenburg lace, and a pretty floral wallpaper complete the warm and welcoming feeling.

Pink candy stripes and Muskoka pine beds greet two lovely young ladies when they visit their grandfather's cottage.

With a mixture of bright pastels, trompe l'oeil, and wicker, Judith Slaughter designed a very imaginative room for her granddaughter.

BOYS WILL BE BOYS

Pam Ernst was asked by her clients to set the decorating wheels in motion around their three-year-old son's new Corvette bed. A unique traffic light lamp highlights the fast-paced decor.

Debra Rose hit a home run when her clients wanted a showcase bedroom for cherished Cincinnati Reds memorabilia and the framed portraits of their sons. A Reds border and striped paper meet at chairrail height.

When the clients of Carol Stearns and Tonya DeMaar, who live on a bay in Florida, asked them to decorate a boy's room, they picked primary colors and a nautical theme. This fun bright room has blue pinstriped paper topped by a border of boats.

The Cincinnati Reds baseball theme and colors were carried right into the clever cornices over gray macro blinds with red tape.

The border of boats, anchor motif fabric, and the unique valances follow through on the nautical theme, and fold back like a sail, displaying bright yellow lining tacked by red buttons.

Along with the Corvette bed, the black-and-white checkered fabric adds to the speedway appearance of this room. An appropriate border ties together two different colorways of the same wallpaper pattern.

DECORATING FOR
TWIN DAUGHTERS

*Sarah's room is full of space saving
ideas, including using one pattern
throughout.*

This is how Ohio interior decorator Kathy Dyer, DDCD, explained one of her favorite projects, "When my twin daughters, Laura and Sarah, were moved into separate rooms, I had the distinct pleasure of decorating two ultra feminine spaces."

Masses of bouquets fill Laura's Victorian inspired bedroom. A coordinating floral panel stripe adorns the valance and bowed bishop sleeves that frame the window. The highlight of the room is an old pine chest which is covered in wallpaper with a matching swagged floral border on each drawer. A great effect at minimal cost.

The appearance of a larger than 9 foot X 11 foot room can be attributed to Kathy's use of one delicate pattern throughout her daughter Sarah's room. Other space-savers are the darling, but practical window seat that is used for daydreaming and clothes storage, and an open bookcase reworked into a bifold closet. A white painted iron and brass daybed minimizes sleeping space, while a skirted and swagged kidney-shaped dressing table adds balance and the extra feminine touch.

*Masses of floral bouquets fill Laura's
Victorian inspired bedroom.*

PRE-TEEN STYLES

Expressions of taste come into play during a girl's pre-teen years. These two young ladies had some definite ideas about how they would like to have their rooms decorated.

Beautiful bright pastel prints create a grown-up aura to this dreamy bedroom created for a 12-year-old California girl. Tonie Vander Hulst designed the whole room around the window, using it as a backdrop for the romantically appointed bed.

A room that would last until their 11-year-old daughter was in her mid-teens was what the client desired. Decorators Pam Ernst and Nancy Greiner of Illinois picked out an engaging border that allows this young lady to continually change the pictures to her fit her growing needs. The choice of solid fabrics keeps the room adaptable and somewhat ageless.

An engaging border allows this young lady to change pictures to fit her growing needs.

*The window became the backdrop
for the romantically appointed bed.*

PURPLE. . .THE CHOICE OF LITTLE PRINCESSES

There is something about the color purple that makes many young girls yearn for a purple bedroom.

Six-year-old aspiring prima ballerina, Jacqueline, is surrounded by her favorite things in a room that would please any purple lover. Texas decorator Carol Eldridge rimmed the room with a colorful border that adds punch to the otherwise monochromatic scheme. On exhibit are a collection of "Dick and Jane" readers, and Wedgwood doll china.

Decorator Terri Ann Parks had two walls of built-in shelves to house her daughter Michele's growing collection of stuffed toys. The shelves' backs were painted a deep purple making the room appear larger. A delicate floral wallpaper border frames the girlish balloon valance. Michele's multi-pillowed daybed has a "pop up" trundle for those sleep-over parties.

The girlish balloon valance is dressed with striped bows and covered buttons.

Decorator Carol Eldridge rimmed the room with a colorful border that adds punch to the otherwise monochromatic scheme.

*Splashes of color decorate a bedroom
for an aspiring artist.*

TEENAGE INDIVIDUALITY

These two looks suit the individual personalities of the young women who live in each of these rooms.

Colorful painterly patterns, sophisticated black, and designer accents befit the teenager who lives in this bedroom. Presently a student majoring in art, the room has been decorated by New Jersey decorator Dawn Hladkey, in a style portraying a young artist. Brilliant splashes of color on the fabric are repeated on a custom area rug. The upscaled bohemian ambience includes a worldly mix of classical elements, like the columned bedside table and pedestal lamp.

Laura Miller's Illinois client wanted to decorate her daughter's bedroom for her 16th birthday. She asked for a multi-purpose design so that the room would function as a guest room when her daughter left for college. The affordable window treatment consists of a striped wallcovering cut into strips for the existing verticals, topped by a pretty fabric turned valance. Restful green walls contrast beautifully with the white furnishings.

A pretty fabric turned valance tops coordinating vertical blinds in this girl's room.

DIVINE DESIGN

For a quick pick-me-up for any room, try a border. It can coordinate with the wallpaper, or accent a painted room. Most often borders outline the ceiling, but the possibilities are limited only by your imagination. It is easy to keep up with growing children, and their changing interests by simply switching border designs.

HOME OFFICES

NOWADAYS ALMOST EVERYONE HAS A FULL TIME, PART TIME, OR SOMETIME OFFICE AT HOME. THE ACCESSIBILITY OF PERSONAL COMPUTERS AND PRINTERS, ALONG WITH THE INFLUX OF AFFORDABLE FACSIMILE AND COPY MACHINES HAS MADE IT POSSIBLE TO RUN AN EFFICIENT OPERATION FROM HOME. ONE OF THE NICER THINGS ABOUT DECORATING YOUR HOME OFFICE IS THAT, UNLESS YOU ARE SHARING, YOU HAVE NO ONE TO PLEASE BUT YOURSELF. MOST DECORATING EXPERIENCES INCLUDE OTHER MEMBERS OF THE FAMILY, OR AT LEAST A CONCERN FOR THE PLEASURE OF OTHERS. BUT YOUR OFFICE CAN BE AS PERSONAL AS YOU WANT IT TO BE. IDEALLY, THE SPACE YOU SELECT SHOULD BE QUIET, PRIVATE, AND AWAY FROM GENERAL HOUSEHOLD ACTIVITY.

FRENCH ACCOMPLI

My home office is housed in a light and airy second floor room that is located down the hall, away from the rest of the bedrooms. It is private and quiet, and large enough to accommodate everything I need to carry out my dual careers of interior decorating and writing.

The decorating direction was inspired by my love of black labs and a fabric that I designed around the stages in a Labrador retriever's life. It is a black-and-white toile that depicts scenes remembered from the eleven years with my devoted dog, Partner. In his honor, I named this fabric, "Partner's Legacy." Decorating Den donates the proceeds from the sale of the fabric to Leader Dogs for the Blind®.

When it came to deciding what to do with the old plaster walls in my office, I borrowed an idea often seen in European homes. The walls were covered with fabric, but with a different twist. Rather than the traditional padding behind the fabric, I had my glorious toile quilted like a bedspread. Quarter inch furring strips were attached to the wall, and the quilted fabric was then stapled to the strips. Double edged self welting adds the finishing touch to rough edges at ceiling.

A treasured reproduction Regence desk with its gentle curves and mellow wood tones also inspired the room's "South of

Louis XV curves meet with a 90's version of Toile de Jouy for my personal version of French Country.

France" ambience. I worked with faux painter Laura Chandler to devise ways to continue the mood on doors, bookcase, and radiator. Fake beams were added to the ceiling. I am particularly fond of large bulletin boards. As a child visiting an exhibit of William Harnett paintings, I remember being fascinated with his trompe l'oeil paintings of cards and letters displayed behind racks of crisscrossed and tacked ribbon. My old cork bulletin board has now been replaced with a romantic black grosgrain rack reminiscent of a Harnett.

Another love of mine is collecting quotes and pithy sayings. I selected my favorites and painted them on a canvas fabric. Most are in English, but I mixed in a few Latin, French, and Spanish phrases. The pieces of canvas were then stitched together to make a cushion and pillows for a Louis XV style bench. Everyday, I get a charge out of seeing these sayings displayed so prominently. A quote that did not make it on the fabric made it onto the bookcase. "Qui me amat, amat et canem meam," Latin for, "Love me, love my dog."

Favorite bits and pieces displayed behind a rack of crisscrossed ribbon.

Bradley on his own toile dog bed, keeping me company. Special sayings cover pillows for a Louis XV bench.

HOME OFFICES THAT WORK

*The soothing spectrum of colors, along
with the desk arrangement, work well
for both husband and wife.*

*Dark geometric wallcovering with coor-
dinating vertical blinds, and a light
Berber carpet totally transformed this
once bland room into "...a knock-out!"*

These contemporary offices use space efficiently. Each one is stamped with the individual personality of its occupants

A Texas scientist, who planned many intense hours editing his next medical book, retained interior decorator Edie Stull, DDCD, to redecorate his family-room-turned-office with some contemporary drama.

Utilizing the existing furniture, Edie picked a "moonlight" color palette...dark and dramatic geometric paper for the walls, with coordinating fabrics for the vertical blinds and valance. A light Berber carpet and newly painted white ceiling complete the transformation.

Kathy Eten, a Kentucky decorator, was challenged to convert a small guestroom into a home office for two which would still be ready for guests. She came up with an open work area with two desks and chairs positioned to accommodate husband and wife, working simultaneously, if necessary. A sofa bed was added for overnight guests. Kathy created a fabric border after her original idea of hiring an artist to replicate the plaid design became too costly.

PROFESSIONAL WOMEN

Here is how two professional women personalized their home office with a sunny color palette. Michigan interior decorator, Carol Sanborn, who suffers from low light syndrome, designed a light, bright office in her basement with furnishings and fabrics in pleasing summer hues, from the floral chintz window swag, to the slipcovered antique chairs and custom-designed round area rug. Instead of built-ins, Carol chose a variety of portable cabinets and chests that can easily be moved to another spot or another house.

Lorna Kyle, Decorating Den's first international franchisee, chose this sunny palette to reflect her Scottish doctor client's vibrant personality and sensitivity to the healthy benefits of cheerful surroundings. No matter how gray the Scottish weather outside, walls and floors have a warm yellow glow, with a hint of honey in the carpeting. Upholstered furniture is covered in a soft mid-tone texture. The beautiful Oriental-inspired fabric frames views of the picturesque Scottish land-scape. Lorna says, "I think you feel better on entering the room, as the colors brighten anyone's day!"

Cherished personal items have been blended into this efficient working office to "...keep me mindful of my past as well as my future," Michigan decorator Carol Sanborn explains.

Glorious sunny colors suit the doctor client's vibrant personality and sensitivity to the healthy benefits of cheerful surroundings.

*Light furniture and pleasing summer
palette give this basement office its
bright appearance.*

REFINED RETREATS

Railroaded upholstery weight fabric creates an unusually luxurious window treatment.

Traditional furniture and colors were selected to enhance the client's art work.

The royal treatment was given to the military epaulet decorated valance.

The main criteria for Ohio decorator Kathy Dyer, DDCD, in decorating this home office was that it be both functional and reflective of her client's interest in military history. Kathy's strategy focused on an innovative gold fringed epaulet treatment for the window valance, and a coat-of-arms border at the ceiling and chair rail

Florida decorator Dot Bushong, DDCD, made the most of an average window for the home office of her client Mindy Myers. Dot designed a fringed box-pleated drapery, mounted on an arched board, and embellished it with brass tacks, ropes, and tassels. A horizontal stripe was achieved by railroading the fabric, using upholstery weight fabric to create a feeling of luxury.

As a birthday present for Dottie Bowen's husband, Missouri interior decorator Susan Eilers, created "...a comfortable office to work in on weekends." Susan picked beige, mulberry, and navy to highlight Mr. Bowen's art work. She used a light textured string wallcovering contrasted with a dark minidot print and a paisley border. The gentle curves of the shade are repeated in the double cord trimmed cornice.

WINDOW TREATMENTS

IT IS ALMOST IMPOSSIBLE TO KEEP UP WITH THE WEALTH OF HARD WINDOW PRODUCTS AVAILABLE TODAY, LET ALONE BE FAMILIAR WITH THE SCOPE OF CUSTOM DRAPERY AND TOP TREATMENT STYLES THAT COULD BE APPROPRIATE FOR YOUR INDIVIDUAL SITUATION. IN THE PAST FEW YEARS WE HAVE SEEN A TREMENDOUS EXPANSION IN THE HARDWARE INDUSTRY (RODS, FINIALS, BRACKETS, TIEBACK HOLDERS). BRASS, WOOD, WROUGHT IRON, PEWTER, AND FABRIC, ARE SOME OF THE CHOICES FOR FINISHES. THROUGHOUT DIVINE DESIGN WE HAVE SHOWN YOU A VARIETY OF STYLES, FROM CLASSIC TO INNOVATIVE, FROM SIMPLE TO SMASHING. ON THE FOLLOWING PAGES YOU WILL SEE A FEW MORE EXAMPLES OF WHY DECORATING DEN IS KNOWN FOR ITS SUPERB WINDOW TREATMENTS.

Knotted swags over layered sheers filter the sun and enhance the 17 foot height of these corner windows.

HIGH DRAMA IN TEXAS

Navy and white stripe swag and cascades over plain side panels give this room a striking contemporary look.

How to handle windows that are the size and proportion of the two featured here can be an overwhelming proposition. But, not to these talented Decorating Den interior decorators.

Carol Hoepfner, DDCD, developed a sophisticated swag banded in navy and white stripes for her client. The matching cascades which hang from a shirred cornice over plain side panels create a soft, but striking, contemporary look.

Beverly Baldwin's clients asked her to enhance the 17 foot corner arch-top windows without hiding them but filtering the morning sun. Shirred panels in a contemporary print frame each window, enhancing the height while knotted swags over layered sheers unify this room's dramatic focal point.

GRACEFUL GATHERINGS

When Michigan decorator Valerie Young was asked to decorate the newly constructed two-story great room of her clients the Goodalls, she came up with a design that suits both Lorri Goodall's traditional taste, and her husband's more contemporary leanings. Quartz-colored tergal batiste sheers fall softly from a shirred ceiling valance. The way the three panels are gracefully tied into bishop's sleeves creates a lovely ethereal quality.

Based on the colorful furniture of Anita Faulkner's client, she designed an elegant window treatment of eyebrow arched formal swags and cascades, using a snow white textured fabric, accent lined in black, over Duettes. The effect is simply smashing!

A snow white textured fabric conforms to the eyebrow arch of the windows for an elegant look.

*Softly draped sheers pleased both
the traditional taste of Lorri Goodall
and the more contemporary leanings
of her husband.*

AUTHENTIC ENGLISH COUNTRY

In decorating the Duxbury's home, Rita Aston found out that there is a price to pay for all that "thatched cottage charm." In addition to the usual uneven walls and floors, the Duxbury's house had barely survived a very bad fire. Rita had the pleasant job of helping to restore this circa 1650 English cottage.

One of her major challenges was the window and door at the end of the chestnut-beamed lounge. The curtains varied as much as two feet from one side of the pair to the other. Rita decided on a shaped valance because if she had opted to do a straight valance it would not have aligned to the window panes, or if she had tried to align it, the beams caused problems. A soft lilac and blue print goes well against the dark beams and white ceilings for a typical English cottage look.

The shaped valance overcame the problem of beams and uneven walls in this charming English cottage.

ASYMMETRICAL ARRANGEMENTS

The popularity of asymmetric informally balanced design is an outgrowth of the trend towards a more relaxed style of decorating. Following the understated tones of the rest of the room Texas decorator Nancy Travis chose a bone textured cotton fabric for the asymmetric one piece drapery, swag and jabot. Lined in wisteria, with a braided tieback to match, the window treatment enhances the pair of long miniblinds.

Ohio decorator Mary Zimmermann, DDCD, took care of all of her client's requests with this muted blue and neutral fabric that covers the windows only where necessary and softens all the straight lines. Each window treatment by itself is asymmetrically designed, but becomes balanced when paired with its partner window.

Interior decorator Barbara Heintze created a serene master bedroom for her Illinois clients. The multi-color abstract print makes up the cleverly lined and knotted swags, hung on fabric-gathered rods over sheers, lined for additional privacy.

Lined sheers are topped with knotted swags hung on fabric-covered rods.

Windows framing the fireplace have been softened with a pair of soft swags. The furniture placement, embellishment on the wreath, and accessory arrangements also contribute to the informal feeling.

The classic asymmetric window treatment enhances the pair of long miniblinds

A divine design softens these long casement windows.

SIMPLY ELEGANT

This lovely corner was made even more inviting once the windows were dressed. Illinois decorator Joan Suzio provided minimal coverage to soften the long casement windows. The design calls for a single swag with no cascades and made as short as possible. Picking up on the colors of the living room, Joan combined rose with teal banding and black cording.

The rich colors of the living room are reflected in the window treatment.

SHOWHOUSES

THE COYOTE POINT MUSEUM AUXILIARY OPENED THE FIRST DECORATOR SHOWHOUSE IN SAN MATEO, CALIFORNIA IN APRIL, 1958. NO ONE COULD HAVE PREDICTED HOW IMMENSELY POPULAR THIS NEW FUND-RAISING PHENOMENON WOULD BECOME. NOW THIRTY-FIVE YEARS LATER, MOST MAJOR CITIES HOLD ONE OR MORE ANNUAL SHOWCASE HOUSES. THE HOMES SELECTED ARE USUALLY MANSIONS WITH A HISTORY, SUCH AS THE "CAROLANDS." IN OTHER AREAS OF THE COUNTRY, NEW HOMES THAT OFFER OUT-OF-THE-ORDINARY FEATURES ARE OFTEN CHOSEN. IN ANY EVENT, THE MAIN ATTRACTION IS SEEING HOW DECORATORS IMAGINATIVELY TREAT THE ROOMS THEY ARE GIVEN. EVERYONE BENEFITS FROM A SHOWCASE HOUSE. THE DECORATORS HAVE A RARE OPPORTUNITY TO EXPOSE THEIR CREATIVITY TO A VAST AND APPRECIATIVE AUDIENCE. THE PUBLIC GETS TO SEE A SHOWHOUSE OF IDEAS AND THE VERY LATEST DESIGN TRENDS. AND AT THE SAME TIME, A WORTHY CAUSE IS BEING HELPED BY THE FUNDS RAISED AT ONE OF THESE EVENTS.

MODEL HOMES

EVEN THOUGH MODEL HOMES, LIKE SHOW-
HOUSES, ARE DECORATED FOR THE ENJOY-
MENT OF THE PUBLIC, THE REASON FOR A
DECORATED MODEL IS TO HELP THE BUILDER
SELL HIS HOUSES, RATHER THAN LEAVE HIS
NEW BARE HOUSE TO THE IMAGINATION OF A

PROSPECTIVE BUYER, THE SMART BUILDER ELICITS THE HELP OF AN INTERIOR DECORATOR

TO CREATE AN ATMOSPHERE THAT THE CUSTOMER CAN RELATE TO. LESS SHOWY AND MORE

REALISTIC THAN A MANSION SHOWHOUSE, BUILDER'S MODELS (PARADE OF HOMES, HOME-

ARAMAS, SAMPLE HOUSES) ALSO EXPOSE THE PUBLIC TO NEW TRENDS AND IDEAS, AND

OFFER MANY INNOVATIVE DECORATING TIPS. GENERALLY ONE DECORATOR OR A TEAM OF

DECORATORS FROM THE SAME COMPANY WORK ON A MODEL HOME PROJECT, INSURING

CONTINUITY OF DESIGN AND COLOR DIRECTION.

THE CAROLANDS SHOWHOUSE

Decorating Den interior decorators were selected out of 200 European and American designers to do a room in the 1991 Hillsborough Decorator Show House. The home, "Carolands," is the largest privately owned residence in America today. The decorators were charged to bring the abandoned 1917 Beaux Arts style home back to its original grandeur. At one time this residence was considered as a possible location for a West Coast White House.

Picking up on the Presidential theme, the decorators featured Decorating Den's exclusive fabric originally designed for the tablecloths at a special luncheon honoring Barbara Bush. This unique multi-colored toile incorporates the former First Lady's trademark pearls, with flowering urns and subtle patriotic motifs.

The walls of this Carolands bedroom were upholstered in a blue damask, and the floors painted with a black-and-white faux marble finish. One of the room's many interesting features is the unique combination of fabrics at the French windows. Among the antiques and fine reproductions is a 1920 Baccarat crystal chandelier. The splendor of this once decaying room has been beautifully restored.

The room was designed around Decorating Den's exclusive "First Lady" fabric.

A SHOWHOUSE & A MODEL

*Pinstripe wallpaper and a deep-toned
paisley border brought out the beauty
of the wood cabinets and trim.*

A team of Upstate New York Decorating Den interior decorators were selected by the Junior League for their annual showhouse in Buffalo. Their challenge was to create a sophisticated design that would appeal to both a man and a woman. A leafy patterned wallpaper inspired by William Morris sets the tone for their luxurious master bathroom. Jewel-toned towels accent the otherwise black and gold color scheme. The end result is a room that is both fresh and new, yet classic and Old Worldly at the same time.

It was the decorator's job to put some pizzaz into this Virginia model home's secondary bath. The builder wanted a masculine look and labeled it the "grandfather's bath." The decorator's choice of contrasting pinstripe wallpaper and deep-toned paisley border brought out the beauty of the wood cabinets and trim. Mirrored walls not only expand the space visually, but double the natural light. The tailored window treatment completes this handsome new bathroom design.

*A leafy patterned wallpaper inspired
by William Morris sets the tone for this
luxurious bathroom.*

SECRET GARDENS

Two beautiful pairs of window designs, one real, below, and one fake, at right, for a Kentucky Showhouse.

Verdant rolling hills can be seen through arched windows in this "get-away" spare bedroom. The decorators hired a local artist to paint a trompe l'oeil scene for their space in a Kentucky Showhouse. Wicker furniture increases the casual, understated mood which is reflective of the rest of the house. Soft swags are kept in place by plaster corbels adding drama to the window design.

A team of Massachusetts interior decorators turned a dark stairway of a 1920's Georgian brick mansion, Davisson House into a pathway to "The Secret Garden." Their imaginative handling of this narrow space was featured at the prestigious Junior League of Boston Decorator's Show House and Garden Tour, 1993. The handpainted wall mural with an antiqued finish echoes Tasha Tudor's original 1912 illustrations for Frances Hodgson Burnett's Secret Garden. A gate was fashioned as a shutter with a rose and vine garland arched over the top of the window. Frances Hodgson Burnett wrote, "It was the sweetest, most mysterious looking place anyone could imagine."

This imaginative handling of a narrow space was featured at the Junior League Show House in Boston.

Attention to detail can be seen in the
lovely valance and draped table.

MODEL HOME TEAMWORK

This kitchen has the latest features, but was decorated with an "old country" flavor.

These award-winning kitchens are the result of Decorating Den's fantastic team spirit. Decorators working together multiply creativity and speed up productivity.

Five Ohio decorators created a comfortable kitchen with enough visual impact to make a lasting impression. They unified the transom windows with a striking fruit print in goldenrod, contrasted with claret and wintergreen triangular handkerchiefs. A cherry paper covers the walls. The iron baker's rack, country furnishings and accessories complete the enticing look.

The decorating goal of the North Carolina team who pooled their talents to do this kitchen, was to reflect the beauty of the spring gardens surrounding the model home. They chose an open ivy print wallpaper to complement the white cabinets and green marble countertops. The clever reverse window valance combines an overall floral fabric with ruby chintz.

Ivy designed wallpaper and a clever reverse valance reflect the outside gardens.

A lovely Victorian wrought iron breakfast set captures a garden mood.

ACCENT ON THE MAN IN THE HOUSE

Two rooms that captivated the thousands of people who paraded through these Southern Ohio model homes were this dual purpose guest/sitting room and the home office. The decorating style of the former is more laid-back and casual, while the latter tends to be traditional and formal.

This dual purpose room is colorful, masculine, and right in tune with the ever popular Western look. Decorating models call for ingenious solutions, such as this simple, but highly effective window treatment where a tree limb was substituted for the standard drapery rod. The twig furnishings emphasize the back-to-nature look, while ocher walls create the perfect backdrop for the vibrant red and blue fabrics. An Indian design border that outlines the angled ceiling tops off a room with comfortable appeal.

Rich wood paneling and floors were the inspiration for the elegant direction of this home office. The decorators chose a light damask wallcovering accented by a beautiful jewel-toned swag border at the ceiling and above the dado. Flanking the handsome fireplace are asymmetrical pole swags trimmed with ivory bullion fringe. Accessories play up the masculine focus of the room, and the entire theme of this golf course home.

Decorated with a business executive/golfer in mind.

Accessories add a homey touch to this model room.

With emphasis on the back-to-nature look, this dual purpose guest/sitting room has a positively Western accent.

"EMPTY NESTER" STYLE

1993 Decorator of the Year Judith Slaughter, DDCD, was asked by her Georgia builder client to furnish a model home for his "empty nesters" target market, who are looking for something smaller and more special when their children are grown.

Wicker, painted furniture, and fresh green-and-white stripes complemented by trailing ivy patterns give the model's family kitchen a relaxed upscale country look. The sitting area around

The fireplace sitting area has a comfortable seating arrangement.

Judith Slaughter's family kitchen portrays an upscaled country look.

the fireplace is small, but a cushy loveseat and chair make it an area to be "lived" in.

Judith decorated the living and dining rooms with light background colors to create the illusion of space for empty nesters who used to entertain in bigger places. But, she accented with strong colors for visual impact, and used furniture arrangements to show ample seating for family gatherings. The Queen Anne furniture, and a mix of checked and floral fabrics provide a traditional, yet relaxed environment. Reds, associated with several holidays, give the room "life" and help create a festive feeling.

Jade walls, simple Country French furniture make the master bedroom feel cozy. Judith made room for a desk and iron framed chair.

Light background, accented with strong colors creates the illusion of space.

Florals and checks mix for a relaxed ambience.

An exotic guest/ sitting room combines
neutrals with black for a highly sophisticated result.

SOOTHING THE PSYCHE

A group of Ohio decorators received multiple awards for their outstanding model home project at Homerama '93.

Together the team designed a stunning guest sitting room. Pellucid tone-on-tone fabrics and wallcoverings provide the foundation of the room. A swirled creme-on-creme fantasy finish covers the walls. Windows and bed are treated to an oversized stripe and a toile print. For contrast, there is a black lacquered antique iron bed with brass fittings, and black drapery poles with gold arrowhead and feather finials. Natural wicker and rattan add textural interest. A final exotic touch of a zebra skin rug contributes to the urbane and au courant ambience of the space.

Mint green painted walls trimmed in white create a refreshing air for this inviting family room. A pair of plaid sofas and reproduction farm style tables create a comfortable conversational area.

The master bedroom is a romantic haven to cushion the clients from the pace and pressures of the outside world. A stylized floral in soft taupe, sage, teal, and plum, and Belgian lace dress the imposing four poster bed. The window treatment was designed to unify three disparate windows and soften the angles of the long wall.

The master bedroom is a statement of refined elegance. The accent stripe adds a somewhat masculine element for balance. A faux finish was applied to the walls for depth and texture.

GROWING UP AND LIKING IT

Any child would like growing up in one of these fabulous rooms. The precious nursery was conceived by a pair of Decorating Den decorators for a Canadian showhouse. Sunny yellow sponged walls, soft pastel prints and frothy sheers seem to float on an ocean of carpet. Duolite Duette shades allow for either light or darkness, or a combination of both, as shown.

With a young lady in mind, Indiana decorators created this darling room. Delicate colors and patterns combine nicely with light and airy wicker furnishings. The knotted and gently falling swag treatment draws attention to the builder's beautiful window and ceiling design.

Very feminine and rich in detail was how a California decorator envisioned this Showhouse bedroom. Stenciled garlands border the walls, while layers of rosy fabrics gather over a lush floral print to make an exquisite backdrop for a young girl's bed.

Sunny yellow and frothy sheers set the stage for some lucky child.

The window treatment draws attention to the builder's beautiful window and ceiling design.

EPILOGUE

Take the Next Step... follow your dreams of becoming an Interior Decorator...

Have you ever dreamed of a career in decorating? Do you have a strong desire to have your own business? Would you enjoy helping people beautify their environments?

If you love to decorate, but need the training to become a professional interior decorator...if you would like to work for yourself, but do not know how to establish your own business...if you think you would derive satisfaction from being part of a system whose mission statement is, "Making the world more beautiful, one room at a time"...perhaps Decorating Den could be the instrument for making your dreams come true.

Decorating Den interior decorators have been teachers, nurses, accountants, managers, salespeople, and secretaries. Some are young mothers, others are single, many are retired seeking a new direction for their lives, some have raised families and now want to do something for themselves, 98 percent are women entrepreneurs, and many are husbands and wives developing a Decorating Den franchise together.

What they all have in common is that they belong to a fantastic franchise system that allows them to work independently while enjoying the benefits and comradeship that come from being a part of a large and expanding international company.

Decorating Den provides its franchisees with ongoing development programs in design, merchandising, and business through our sixty regional centers across the United States, Canada, Scotland, England, Spain, Japan and at our Corporate Offices and Training Facilities in Metropolitan Washington D.C.

The unique Decorating Den ColorVan®, the mobile store that carries thousands of samples to the customer, is revolutionizing the profession of interior decorating. There is an unprecedented demand by the public for a comfortable and affordable way to decorate homes and offices, and Decorating Den is at the forefront of fulfilling that need.

"Growth is key to our future. People are key to our growth. We continue to search for those who want to grow personally, and who want to grow with their own business...people driven by a vision...who want to share in the most beautiful business in the world," says Decorating Den President, Jim Bugg.

For more information on Decorating Den, and how to contact the one closest you, call 1-800-428-1366 ext. 1157 or 301-652-6393.

DECORATOR CREDITS

PHOTOGRAPHER CREDITS